THE INVISIBLE CENSOR

THE INVISIBLE CENSOR

By FRANCIS HACKETT

Essay Index Reprint Series

Originally published by:

B. W. HUEBSCH, INC.

BOOKS FOR LIBRARIES PRESS, INC.
FREEPORT, NEW YORK

First Published 1921
Reprinted 1968

LIBRARY OF CONGRESS CATALOG CARD NUMBER:
68-22093

TO

MY WIFE

SIGNE TOKSVIG

WHOSE LACK OF INTEREST
IN THIS BOOK HAS BEEN MY
CONSTANT DESPERATION

These sketches and articles appeared in the *New Republic* and I am indebted to the other editors for being allowed to reprint them.

CONTENTS

THE INVISIBLE CENSOR

NOT long ago I met a writer who happened to apply the word " cheap " to Mr. Strachey's Eminent Victorians. It astonished me, because this was an erudite, cultivated woman, a distinguished woman, and she meant what she said.

A " cheap " effect, I assume, is commonly one that builds itself on a false foundation. It may promise beautifully, but it never lives up to its promise. Whether it is a house or a human character, a binding or a book, it proves itself gimcrack and shoddy. It hasn't the goods. And of Eminent Victorians, as I remembered it (having read it to review it), this was the last thing to be said. The book began by fitting exquisitely, but it went on fitting exquisitely. It never pulled or strained. And the memory of it wears like a glove.

Now why, after all, did I like this book so thoroughly, which my distinguished friend thought so cheap? For many minor reasons of course, as one likes anything — contributory reasons — but principally, as I laboriously analyzed it, because in Eminent Victorians the invisible censor was so perfectly understood. What seemed cheap to her ladyship was, I do not doubt, the very thing that made Eminent Victorians seem so precious to me — the deft disregard of appearances, the refusal to let decorum stand in the way of our possessing the facts. This to my critic was a proof that Mr. Strachey was imperceptive and vulgar —" common " the ugly word is. To me it simply proved that he knew his game. What he definitely disregarded, as so many felt, was not any decorum dear and worth having. It was simply that decorum which to obey is to produce falsification. The impeccable craft of Mr. Strachey was shown in his evaluation, not his acceptance, of decorum. He did not take his characters at their face value, while he did not do the other vulgar thing, go through their careers with a muck-rake. In vivisecting them (the awful thing to do, presumably), he never let them die on him. He opened them out, but not cruelly or brutally. He did it as Mr. William Johnston plays tennis or as Dr. Blake is said to operate or as Dr. Muck conducts an orchestra or as Miss Kellerman dives. He did it for the best result under the circumstances and with a form that comes of a real command of the medium — genuine " good form."

The essential achievement of Eminent Victorians is worth dwelling on because in every book of social character the question of the invisible censor is unavoidably present. By the censor I do not mean that poor blinkered government official who decides on the facts that are worthy of popular acquaintance. I mean a still more secret creature of still more acute solicitude, who feels that social facts must be manicured and pedicured before they are fit to be seen. He is not concerned with the facts themselves but with their social currency. He is the supervisor of what we say we do, the watchman over our version and our theoretical estimate of ourselves. His object, as I suppose, is to keep up the good old institutions, to set their example before the world, to govern the imitative monkey in us. And to fulfill that object he continually revises and blue-pencils the human legend. He is constantly at the elbow of every man or woman who writes. An invisible, scarcely suspected of existing, he is much more active, much more solidly intrenched, than the legal censor whom liberals detest.

Every one is now more or less familiar with the Freudian censor, the domesticated tribal agent whose function it seems to be to inforce the tribal scruples and superstitions — to keep personal impulse where the tribe thinks it belongs. This part of the ego — to give it a spatial name — came in for a good deal of excited remonstrance in the early days of popular Freudian talk. To-day, I think, the censor is seldom so severely interpreted. In many cases there is clearly a savagery or a stupidity which brings about " the balked disposition," but it is being admitted that the part which is regulated by the censor, the " disposition " end of the ego, may not always be socially tolerable; and as for the " balking," there is a difference between blunt repressiveness and enlightened regulation. Still, with all this acceptance of ethics, the nature of the censorship has to be recognized — the true character of the censor is so often not taste or conscience in any clear condition, but an uninstructed agency of herd instinct, an institutional bully. In the censor as he appears in psycho-analytic literature there is something of the archaic, the irrational and the ritualistic — all just as likely to ask for decorum for themselves as is the thing in us which is against license and anarchy.

In the censor for whom I am groping, the censor

[3]

of whom Eminent Victorians is so subversive, there are particularly these irrational and ritualistic characteristics, these remnants of outgrown institutions, these bondages of race and sex, of class and creed. Most biography, especially official biography, is written with such a censor in mind, under his very eye. Where Eminent Victorians was refreshing and stumulating was precisely in its refusal to keep him in mind. Hovering behind Eminent Victorians we see agonized official biography, with its finger on its lips, and the contrast is perhaps the chief delight that Mr. Strachey affords. When Cardinal Manning's pre-clerical marriage, for example, came to be considered by Mr. Strachey, he did not obey the conventional impulse, did not subordinate that fact of marriage as the Catholic Church would wish it to be subordinated (as a matter of "good taste," of course). He gave to that extremely relevant episode its due importance. And so Manning, for the first time for most people, took on the look not so much of the saintly cardinal of official biography as of a complex living man.

What does the censor care for this æsthetic result? Very little. What the censor is chiefly interested in is, let us say, edification. He aims by no means to give us access to the facts. He aims not at all to let us judge for ourselves. With all his might he strives to relate the facts under his supervision to the end that he thinks desirable, whatever it may be. And so, when facts come to light which do not chime in with his prepossession, he does his best either to discredit them or to set them down as immoral, heretical or contrary to policy. And the policy that he is serving is not æsthetic.

A theory of the æsthetic is now beside the point, but I am sure it would move in a relation to human impulses very different from the relation of the censor. The censor is thinking, presumably, of immediate law and order, with its attendant conventions and respectabilities. The æsthetic could not be similarly bound. It is not reckless of conduct, but surely enormously reckless of decorum, with its conventions and respectabilities clustering around the status quo. Hence the apparent " revolt " of modernism, the insurrection of impulse against edification.

But there is more in Eminent Victorians than an amusing, impish refusal to edify. There is the instructive contrast between the " censored celebrity " and the uncensored celebrity disinterestedly observed. Disinterestedly observed, for one thing, we get something in these celebrities besides patriotism and mother-love and chastity and heroism. We get hot impulses and cold calculations, brandy and treachery, the imperious and the supine, glorious religiousness and silly family prayers. And these things, though very unlike the products of official photography, are closely related to impulses as we know them in ourselves. To find them established for Mr. Strachey's " eminent " Victorians is to enjoy a constant dry humor, since the invisible censor, the apostle of that expediency known as edification, stood at the very heart of Victorianism.

This is possibly why Samuel Butler, in his autobiographical way, is so remarkable as a Victorian. In the midst of innumerable edifying figures, he declined to edify. When people said to him, " Honor thy father and thy mother," he answered in effect that his father was a pinhead theologian who had wanted to cripple his mentality, and his mother was, to use his own phrase, full of the seven deadly virtues. This was not decorous but it had the merit of being true. And all the people whose unbidden censors had been forcing good round impulses into stubborn parental polygons immediately felt the relief of this revelation. Not all of them confess it. When they have occasion to speak or write about "mothers"— as if the biological act of parturition brings with it an unquestionable "mother" psyche — most of them still allow the invisible censor to govern them and represent them as having feelings not really their own. But even this persistence of the censor could not deprive Samuel Butler of his effectiveness. He has spoken out, regardless of edification, and that sort of work cannot be undone.

A similar work is performed by such highly personal confessants as Marie Bashkirtseff and W. N. P. Barbellion, and even by Mary MacLane. The account that these impulsive human beings give of themselves is sensational simply because it clashes with the strict preconception that we are taught to establish. But only a man who remembers nothing or admits nothing of his own impulses can deny the validity of theirs. The thing that takes away from their interest, as one grows older, is the unimportance of the censorship that agonizes them. Their documentary value being their great value, they lose importance as more specific and dramatic documents become familiar. And with psycho-analysis there has been a huge increase in the evidence of hidden life. It is the Montaignes who remain, the confessants who offer something besides a psychological document — a transcendence which is not incoherent with pain.

But these various confessions are significant. They indicate the existence and the vitality of the censor. They show that in the simplest matters we have not yet attained freedom of speech. Why? Because, I imagine, the world is chockful of assumptions as to conduct which, while irrational and ritualistic and primitive, have all sorts of sanctions thrown around them and must take a whole new art of education to correct. Until this art it established and these assumptions are automatically rectified, it will be impossible to exercise free speech comfortably. An attempt may be made, of course, and indeed must be made, but to succeed too well will for many years mean either being exterminated or being ostracized.

It is not hard to show how each of us in turn becomes an agent of the invisible censorship. You, for instance, may have a perfectly free mind on the subject of suffrage, but you may have extremely strong views on the subject of sex. (Miss Alice Stone Blackwell, to be specific, thinks that Fielding is nothing but a " smutty " author.) Or you may think yourself quite emancipated on the subject of sex-desires and be hopelessly intolerant on the subject of the Bolsheviki. The French Rights of Man held out, after all, for the sacred rights of property — and the day before that, it was considered pretty advanced to believe in the divine right of kings. It is not humanly possible, considering how relative liberalism is, to examine all the facts or even convince oneself of the necessity of examining them, and in every case we are sure to be tempted to oppose certain novel ideas in the name of inertia, respectability and decorum. To dissemble awkward facts, in such cases, is much easier than to account for them — which is where the censor comes in.

I do not say that it is possible to do away with every discipline, even the rule-of-thumb of decorum. As a subservient middle-class citizen, I believe in the regulation of impulse. But as an intellectual fact, the use of the blue pencil in the interests of decorum is exceedingly inept. Human impulses are much too lively to be extinguished by the denial of expression. And if sane expression is denied to them, they'll find expression of another kind.

Decorum has its uses, especially on the plane of social intercourse. I admit this all the more eagerly because I have seen much of one brilliant human being who has practically no sense of opposition. If he sees something that he wants, he helps himself. It may be the milk on the lunch-table that was intended for Uncle George. It may be the new volume from England that it took nine weeks to bring across. It may be the company of some sensitive gentlewoman or the busy hour of the mayor of Chicago. The object makes no visible difference to my friend. If he wants it, he sticks out his hand and takes it. And if it comes loose, he holds on.

Associated with this aggressiveness there is a good deal of purpose not self-regarding. The man is by no means all greedy maw. But the thing that distinguishes him is the quickness and frankness with which he obeys his impulse. Between having an impulse and acting on it there lies for him a miraculously short time.

In dealing with such a man, most people begin hilariously. Not all of them keep up with him in the same heroic spirit. At first it is extraordinarily stimulating to find a person who is so " creative," who sweeps so freely ahead. Soon the dull obligations, the tedious details, begin to accumulate, and the man with the happy impulsiveness leaves all these dull obligations to his struggling friends. His lack of decorum in these respects is a source of hardship and misunderstanding, especially where persons of less energy or more circumspection are attendant. In his case, I admit, I see the raw problem of impulse, and I am glad to see his impulse squelched.

But even this barbarian is preferable to the apathetic repressed human beings by whom he is surrounded. Harnessed to the right interests, he is invaluable because " creative." And he should never be blocked in: he should at most be canalled.

The evil of the censor, at any rate, is never illustrated in his rational subordination of impulse, but in those subordinations that violate human and social freedom. And the worst of them are the filmy, the vague, the subtle subordinations that take away the opportunity of truth. Life is in itself a sufficiently difficult picture-puzzle, but what chance have we if the turnip-headed censor confiscates some particularly indispensable fragment that he chooses to dislike? On reading Eminent Victorians, how we rejoice to escape from those wax effigies that we once believed to be statesmen — the kind of effigies of which text-books and correct histories and correct biographies are full! How we rejoice to escape from them, wondering that they had ever imposed on us, wondering that teachers and pious families and loyal historians ever lent themselves to this conspiracy against truth! But the horrible fact is, Mr. Strachey is one in a million. He has only poked his finger through the great spider-web of so-called " vital lies."

Meanwhile, in the decorous and respectable biographies, the same old " vital lies " are being told. The insiders, the initiated, the disillusioned, are aware of them. They no longer subsist on them. They read between the lines. And yet when the insiders see in print the true facts — say, about Robert Louis Stevenson or Swinburne or Meredith or John Jones — these very insiders rush forward with a Mother Hubbard to fling around the naked truth. We must not speak the truth. We must edify. We must bring our young into a spotless, wax-faced world.

It means that we need a revolution in education, nothing less. It means that the truth must be taken out of the hands of the censor. We must be prepared to shed oceans of ink.

WHISKY

IT was a wet, gusty night and I had a lonely walk home. By taking the river road, though I hated it, I saved two miles, so I sloshed ahead trying not to think at all. Through the barbed wire fence I could see the racing river. Its black swollen body writhed along with extraordinary swiftness, breathlessly silent, only occasionally making a swishing ripple. I did not enjoy looking at it. I was somehow afraid.

And there, at the end of the river road where I swerved off, a figure stood waiting for me, motionless and enigmatic. I had to meet it or turn back.

It was a quite young girl, unknown to me, with a hood over her head, and with large unhappy eyes.

" My father is very ill," she said without a word of introduction. " The nurse is frightened. Could you come in and help? "

There was a gaunt house set back from the road, on a little slope. I could see a wan light upstairs.

"The nurse is not scared," the girl corrected, " but she is nervous. I wish you could come."

"Of course," and on my very word she turned and led the way in.

The hall was empty. It had nothing in it except a discouraged oil lamp on a dirty kitchen table. The shadowy stairs were bare. On my left on the ground floor a woman with gray hair and rusty face

[11]

and red-rimmed eyes shuffled back into the shadows at my entry, a sort of ignoble Niobe.

"That's my mother," the grave child explained. And to the retreating slatternly figure the child called, "This man has come to help, Mother," as if men dropped from the sky.

She went up into the shadows and I followed. A flight of stairs, a long creaking landing. Another flight of stairs. Stumbles. Another landing. A stale aroma of cat. And a general sense that, although the staircase was well made and the landings wide, there was not one stick of furniture in the house.

As we approached the top floor we met fresher air and the pallid emanation of a night-light. A figure stood waiting at the head of the stairs.

This was a stout little nun, her face framed in creaking linen, and a great rustle of robes and rosary beads whenever she moved. She began a sharp whisper the minute we climbed to the landing.

"He's awake. He's out of his head. I'm glad you've come. Now, child, be off to bed with you, like a good girl. This way, if you please."

The child's vast eyes accepted me. "I'll go to Mother," she said, and she receded downstairs. The nun entered an open door to the right, and again I meekly followed.

It was a room out of the fables. There was a tall fireplace facing the door, with a slat of packing-case burning in it as well as the wind would permit, and a solitary candle glimmering in a bottle, set on the table at the head of the bed. Its uncertain light fell on the tousled hair of a once kempt human being, now evidently a semi-maniac staring at presences in the room. Down the chimney the wind came bluffing at intervals, and the one high window querulously rattled. The center of the room was the sick man's burning eyes.

I walked through his view and he did not see me. The nun and myself stood watching him from the head of the bed.

" Oh, he's awful bad, you have no idea how bad he is; I'm afraid for him; I am indeed. What am I to call you, Mister? Here, take this chair."

Before I answered her she continued, in a whisper that slid along from one *s* to the next. " They said the doctor would be here at seven and it's nearly twelve as it is. He's not coming. I wish he was here."

The sick man seemed to see us. " That's right now," he said, whistling his breath. " Bring me my clothes, I want to go home."

The nun laid her arm on him. " Lean back now, dear, and it'll be all right, I'm telling you." And she gently but ineffectually tried to press him down.

The sick man turned his face on her, into the candlelight. He was long unshaved, but the two things that struck me most, after the crop of gray bristle, were the dry cavern of his mouth and the scalding intensity of his eyes. I was terrified lest those eyes should alight on me, and yet I gazed hard at him. His lips were flaked with yellow scales, and dry mucus was in strings at the corners of his mouth. His night-shirt gaped open, showing a very hairy black chest. He seemed a shrunken man, not a very tall man, but his shoulders were broad and his chin very square. To support his chin seemed the great effort of his jaws. It fell open on him, giving him a vacant foolish expression, with his teeth so black and irregular, and he tried his best to clamp his teeth tight. The working of his jaws, however, scarcely interfered with his whistling breath or his gasping words.

"They will be at the back door, I say. God!" a feeble scream and whimper. "Bring me my clothes. You're hiding them on me. Oh, why are you hiding them on me? Can't you give me my clothes?"

"You're home now, dear. You're home now," the nurse assured him. "Isn't that your own clock on the mantel? Lie down now and I'll make you a comfortable drink and put you to sleep."

"Boy, fetch me my coat."

"Don't mind him," the nun turned to me, "but do you cover his feet."

His feet had lost the gray blanket. They stared blankly up from the end of the bed. I covered them snugly, glad to have something to do.

"It's all the whisky in him," the nun whispered when at last he went limp and lay down. "It's got to his brain. I thought he was over the pneumonia, but that whisky has him saturated. The poor thing! The poor thing!"

"Well, I must be going now," the sick man ejaculated, and with one twist of his body he was out of bed.

"Oh, keep yourself covered, for the love of God!" The poor nun ran after him with the blanket as his old flannel night shirt fluttered up his legs.

He staggered up to me fiercely, and his eyes razed my face.

"Fiddle your grandmother," he muttered, "I'm off home, I tell you."

"You can't leave the room; it's better for you to go back to bed," and I held him round with my arms.

"See here, you," his yellow cheeks reddened with his passionate effort, "you can't hold me a prisoner any longer. Oh, Barrett, Barrett, what are you doing to me to destroy me?"

I knew no Barrett, but the poor creature was shivering with anguish and cold. I put my arms around him and tried to move him out of the draught of the door. His thin arms closed on me at the first hint of force, and he clenched with feverish vigor. I could feel his frail bones against me, his bare ribs, his wild thumping heart.

"You can't, you can't. You can't keep me prisoner. . . ."

He struggled, his heart thumping me. Then in one instant he went slack.

We lifted him to the bed, and I felt under his shirt for the flutter of his heart. His mouth had dropped open, his eyes were like a dead bird's.

The little nun began, "Jesus, Mary and Joseph," and other holy words, while I groped helplessly over this fragile burned-out frame. Then I remembered and I stumbled wild-minded to find that woman downstairs.

I went headlong through the darkness. At my knock the door opened, as if by an unseen hand, and I saw, completely dressed, the pale little girl, with her grave eyes.

"Your mother?" I asked.

The child stopped me sharply, "Is Father worse?"

"He's worse," I answered feebly. "You'd better —"

The child was brushed aside by her mother, who had stumbled forward from inside. She looked at me vaguely.

The girl turned on her mother. "I'm going up to Father. Go inside."

The woman's will flickered and then expired. She pulled the door back upon herself, shutting us into the hall. The child led and I followed back upstairs.

BILLY SUNDAY, SALESMAN

I

BEFORE I heard Billy Sunday in Philadelphia
I had formed a conception of him from the newspapers. First of all, he was a baseball player become revivalist. I imagined him as a ranting,
screaming vulgarian, a mob orator who lashed himself and his audience into an ecstasy of cheap religious fervor, a sensationalist whose sermons were
fables in slang. I thought of him as vividly, tor-
rentially abusive, and I thought of his revival as an
orgy in which hundreds of sinners ended by streaming in full view to the public mourners' bench.
With the penitents I associated the broken humanity
of Magdalen, disheveled, tearful, prostrate, on her
knees to the Lord. I thought of Billy Sunday pre-
siding over a meeting that was tossed like trees in
a storm.

However this preconception was formed, it at
least had the merit of consistency. It was, that is
to say, consistently inaccurate in every particular.

Consider, in the first place, the orderliness of his
specially constructed Tabernacle. Built like a giant
greenhouse in a single story, it covers an immense
area and seats fifteen thousand human beings.
Lighted at night by electricity as if by sunshine, the
floor is a vast garden of human faces, all turned

to the small platform on which the sloping tiers from behind converge. Around this auditorium, with its forest of light wooden pillars and braces, runs a glass-inclosed alley, and standing outside in the alley throng the spectators for whom there are no seats. Except for the quiet ushers, the silent sawdust aisles are kept free. Through police-guarded doors a thin trickle fills up the last available seats, and this business is dispatched with little commotion. Fully as many people wait to hear this single diminutive speaker as attend a national political convention. In many ways the crowd suggests a national convention; but both men and women are hatless, and their attentiveness is exemplary.

It is, if the phrase is permitted, conspicuously a middle-class crowd. It is the crowd that wears Cluett-Peabody collars, that reads the Ladies' Home Journal and the Saturday Evening Post. It is the crowd for whom the nickel was especially coined, the nickel that pays carfare, that fits in a telephone slot, that buys a cup of coffee or a piece of pie, that purchases a shoe-shine, that pays for a soda, that gets a stick of Hershey's chocolate, that made Woolworth a millionaire, that is spent for chewing-gum or for a glass of beer. In that crowd are men and women from every sect and every political party, ranging in color from the pink of the factory superintendent's bald head to the ebony of the discreetly dressed negro laundress. A small proportion of professional men and a small proportion of ragged labor is to be discerned, but the general tone is simple, common-sense, practical, domestic America. Numbers of young girls who might equally well be at the movies are to be seen, raw-boned boys not long from the country, angular home-keeping virgins of the sort that belong to sewing circles, neat young men who suggest the Y. M. C. A., iron-gray mothers who recall the numbered side-streets in Harlem or Brooklyn or Chicago West Side and who bring to mind asthma and the price of eggs, self-conscious young clerks who are half curious and partly starved for emotion, men over forty with prominent Adam's apple and the thin, strained look of lives fairly care-worn and dutiful, citizens of the kind that with all their heterogeneousness give to a jury its oddly characteristic effect, fattish men who might be small shopkeepers with a single employee, the single employee himself, the pretty girl who thinks the Rev. Mr. Rhodeheaver so handsome, the prosaic girl whose chief perception is that Mr. Sunday is so hoarse, the nervously facetious youths who won't be swayed, the sedentary "providers" who cannot open their ears without dropping their jaws. A collection of decidedly stable, normal, and one may crudely say "average" mortals, some of them destined to catch religion, more of them destined to catch an impression, and a few of them, sitting near the entrances, destined resentfully to catch a cold.

Very simple and pleasant is the beginning. Mr. Sunday's small platform is a bower of lovely bouquets, and the first business is the acknowledgment of these offerings. As a means of predisposing the audience in Mr. Sunday's favor nothing could be more genial. In the body of the hall are seated the sponsors of these gifts, and as each tribute is presented to view, Mr. Rhodeheaver's powerful, commonplace voice invites them to recognition:

"Is the Pittsburgh Plate Glass Company here?"
All eyes turn to a little patch of upstanding brethren.
"Fine, fine. We're glad to see yeh here. We're
glad to welcome yeh. And what hymn would *you*
like to have?" In loud concert the Pittsburgh
Plate Glass Co. delegation shout: "Number forty-
nine!" Mr. Rhodeheaver humorously parodies the
shout: "Number forty-nine! It's a good 'un too.
Thank yeh, we're glad to have yeh here." Not only
immense bouquets, but gold pieces, boxes of hand-
kerchiefs, long mirrors, all sorts of presents, mainly
from big corporations or their employees, are on
the tight platform. One present came from a mill,
a box of towels, and with it not only a warm, manly
letter asking Mr. Sunday to accept "the product
of our industry," but a little poetic tribute, express-
ing the hope that after his strenuous sermon Mr.
Sunday might have a good bath and take comfort
in the use of the towels. Every one laughed and
liked it, and gazed amiably at the towels.

The hymns were disappointing. If fifteen thousand people had really joined in them the effect
would have been stupendous. As it was, they were
thrilling, but not completely. The audience was
not half abandoned enough.

Then, after a collection had been taken up for a
local charity, Mr. Sunday began with a prayer. A
compact figure in an ordinary black business suit,
it was instantly apparent from his nerveless voice
that, for all his athleticism, he was tired to the
bone. He is fifty-three years old and for nine
weeks he had been delivering about fifteen extremely
intense sermons a week. His opening was almost

adramatic. It had the conservatism of fatigue, and it was only his evident self-possession that canceled the fear he would fizzle.

The two men whom Sunday most recalled to me at first were Elbert Hubbard and George M. Cohan. In his mental caliber and his pungent philistinism of expression he reminded me of Hubbard, but in his physical attitude there was nothing of that greasy orator. He was trim and clean-cut and swift. He was like a quintessentially slick salesman of his particular line of wares.

Accompanying one of the presents there had been a letter referring to Billy Sunday's great work, "the moral uplift so essential to the business and commercial supremacy of this city and this country." As he developed his homely moral sermon for his attentive middle-class congregation, this gave the clew to his appeal. It did not seem to me that he had one touch of divine poetry. He humored and argued and smote for Christ as a commodity that would satisfy an enormous acknowledged gap in his auditors' lives. He was "putting over" Christ. In awakening all the early memories of maternal admonition and counsel, the consciousness of unfulfilled desires, of neglected ideals, the ache for sympathy and understanding, he seemed like an insurance agent making a text of "over the hill to the poorhouse." He had at his finger tips all the selling points of Christ. He gave to sin and salvation a practical connotation. But while his words and actions apparently fascinated his audience, while they laughed eagerly when he scored, and clapped him warmly very often, to me he appealed no more than an ingenious electric advertisement, a bottle picked out against the darkness pouring out a foaming glass of beer.

And yet his heart seemed to be in it, as a salesman's heart has to be in it. Speaking the language of business enterprise, the language with which the great majority were familiar, using his physical antics merely as a device for clinching the story home, he gave to religion a great human pertinence, and he made the affirmation of faith seem creditable and easy. And he defined his own object so that a child could understand. He was a recruiting officer, not a drill sergeant. He spoke for faith in Christ; he left the rest to the clergy. And to the clergy he said: " If you are too lazy to take care of the baby after it is born, don't blame the doctor."

It was in his platform manners that Sunday recalled George M. Cohan. When you hear that he goes through all the gyrations and gesticulations of baseball, you think of a yahoo, but in practice he is not wild. Needing to arrest the attention of an incredibly large number of people, he adopts various evolutions that have a genuine emphatic value. It is a physical language with which the vast majority have friendly heroic associations, and for them, spoken so featly and gracefully, it works. Grasping the edge of the platform table as if about to spring like a tiger into the auditorium, Sunday gives to his words a drive that makes you tense in your seat. Whipping like a flash from one side of the table to the other, he makes your mind keep unison with his body. He keys you to the pitch that the star baseball player keys you, and although you stiffen when he flings out the name of Christ as if he were sending a spitball right into your teeth, you realize it is only an odd, apt, popular conventionalization of the ordinary rhetorical gesture. Call it his bag of tricks, deem it incongruous and stagey, but if Our Lady's Juggler is romantic in grand opera, he is not a whit more romantic than this athlete who has adapted beautiful movements to an emphasis of convictions to which the audience nods assent.

The dissuading devil was conjured by Sunday in his peroration, and then he ended by thanking God for sending him his great opportunity, his vast audience, his bouquets and his towels. When he finished, several hundred persons trailed forward to shake hands and confess their faith — bringing the total of " penitents " up to 35,135.

Bending with a smile to these men and women who intend to live in the faith of Christ, Billy Sunday gives a last impression of kindliness, sincerity, tired zeal. And various factory superintendents and employers mingle benignly around, glad of a religion that puts on an aching social system such a hot mustard plaster.

II

Oyster soup is a standard item in the money-making church supper. The orphan oyster searching vainly for a playmate in an ocean of church soup is a favorite object of Billy Sunday's pity. He loves to caricature the struggling church, with its time-serving, societyfied, tea-drinking, smirking preachers. " The more oyster soup it takes to run a church," he shouts sarcastically, " the faster it runs to the devil."

[23]

An attitude so scornful as this may seem highly unconventional to the outsider. It leads him to think that Billy Sunday is a radical. The agility with which the Rev. Billy climbs to the top of his pulpit and then pops to the platform on all fours suggests a corresponding mental agility. He must be a dangerous element in the church, the outsider imagines; he must be a religious revolutionary. And then the outsider beholds John Wanamaker or John D. Rockefeller, Jr., on the platform alongside the revivalist — pillars of society, prosperous and respectable gentlemen who instinctively know their business.

Fond as his friends are of comparing Billy Sunday to Martin Luther or John the Baptist, none of them pushes the comparison on the lines of radicalism, and Sunday himself waives the claim to being considered revolutionary. "I drive the same kind of nails all orthodox preachers do," he says in one of his sermons. "The only difference is that they use a tack hammer and I use a sledge." No one supposes that Martin Luther could have said this. Sledge-hammer orthodoxy was not exactly the distinguishing characteristic of Martin Luther. The conservatism of Billy Sunday's message is the first fact about him. Where he differs from the orthodox preacher is not in his soul but in his resolution. He has the mind of Martin Tupper rather than of Martin Luther, but it is combined with that competent American aggressiveness which one finds in a large way in George M. Cohan, Theodore Roosevelt, even Ty Cobb. Theology does not interest Billy Sunday. He compares it to ping-pong and compares himself to a jack-rabbit and says he knows as little about theology as a jack-rabbit knows about ping-pong. What he cares about is religious revival. He knows the church is in bitter need of revival. He is out to administer digitalis, in his own phrase, instead of oyster soup.

For many years the church has been waning, and Billy Sunday scorns the effeminate, lily-handed efforts at resuscitation that the churchmen have employed. To put pepperino into a religious campaign, to make Christianity hum, requires more than cushioned pews, extra music, coffee and macaroons. Had Billy Sunday been in the regular theatrical business he would not have fussed with a little independent theatre. He would have conducted a Hippodrome. To rival the profane world's attractions he sees no reason for rejecting the profane world's methods. So tremendous an object as curing an institution's pernicious anæmia justifies the most violent, outrageous experiment.

If Jesus Christ were a new automobile or an encyclopædia or a biscuit, Billy Sunday would have varied the method he has employed in putting Him over, but he would not have varied the spirit of his revival-enterprise in any essential particular. His object, as he sees it, is to sell Christ. It is an old story that from its economic organization society takes its complexion. The Sunday revival takes its complexion from business enterprise without a single serious change. There is one great argument running all through Billy Sunday's sermons — the argument that salvation will prove a profitable investment — but much more clearly derived from business than the ethics preached by Billy Sunday is the method he has devised for promoting Jesus Christ. Even the quarrel between " Ma " Sunday and the man who has lost the post-card concession is an illustration of the far-reaching efficiency of the system. The point is not that money is being made out of the system. " An effort to corrupt Billy Sunday," to use a paraphrase, " would be a work of supererogation, besides being immoral." If Billy Sunday has a large income, $75,000 or $100,000 a year, it is not because he is mercenary. It is only because a large income is part of the natural fruits of his promoting ability. Left to himself, it is quite unlikely that Billy Sunday would care a straw about his income, beyond enough to live well and to satisfy his vanity about clothes. It is Mrs. Sunday who sees to it that her promoter-husband is not left penniless by those Christian business men who so delightedly utilize his services.

The backbone of Billy Sunday's success is organization. When organization has delivered the crowd, Billy is ready to sweat for it and spit for it and war-whoop for it and dive for base before the devil can reach him. He is ready to have " Rody " come on the programme with his slide-trombone and to have any volunteer who wishes to do it hit the sawdust-trail. But he does not let his success depend on any programme. His audiences are, in great measure, contracted for in advance. It is in grasping the necessity for this kind of preparedness, in taking from the business world its lessons as to canvassing and advertising and standardizing the goods, that Billy can afford to jeer at oyster soup. As his authorized biographer complacently says, " John the Baptist was only a voice: but Billy Sunday is a voice, plus a bewildering array of committees and assistants and organized machinery. He has committees galore to coöperate in his work: a drilled Army of the Lord. In the list of Scranton workers that is before me I see tabulated an executive committee, the directors, a prayer-meeting committee, an entertainment committee, an usher committee, a dinner committee, a business women's committee, a building committee, a nursery committee, a personal worker's committee, a decorating committee, a shop-meetings committee — and then a whole list of churches and religious organizations in the city as ex officio workers!" In New York on April 9th there was a private meeting of 7,000 personal workers, " another step in the direction of greasing the campaign."

Unless Billy Sunday had some skill as a performer he naturally could not hold his place as a revivalist. His success consists largely, however, in the legendary character that has been given him by all the agencies that seek to promote this desperate revival of orthodox religion. His acrobatic stunts on the platform are sufficiently shocking to make good publicity. His much-advertised slang, repeated over and over, has a similar sensational value. But the main point about him is the dramatization of his own personality. His virility is perhaps his chief stock-in-trade. No one, not Mr. Roosevelt himself, has insisted so much on his personal militant masculinity. Although well over fifty, his youthful prowess as a baseball-player is still a headline-item in his story, and every sermon he preaches gives him a chance to prove he is physically fit. In addition to this heroic characteristic there is his fame as a self-made man. He is a plain man of the people, as he never fails to insist. He carries " the malodors of the barnyard " with him. But he has succeeded. The cost of his special tabernacle is one of his big distinctions. The size of his collections is another. His personal fortune, in spite of all criticism, is a third. Besides these heroic attributes of strength and wealth there is his melodramatic simplicity of mind. All of his sermons are " canned " and a great deal of the material in them is borrowed, but he manages to deliver his message straight from the shoulder, as if it were his own. There can be no doubt that his shouting, his slang, his familiarity with Jesus, his buttonholing old God, his slang-version of the Bible, do offend large numbers of people. They arrest attention so successfully, even in these cases, that they turn out to be well advised. There is nothing spontaneous about these antics. They are switched on at the beginning of a revival and switched off as it succeeds. They are Sunday's native way of lighting up the strait and narrow path with wriggling electric signs.

Billy Sunday has too much energy to stick completely fast in the mud of conservatism. He is capable of advocating sex instruction for the young, for example, and he permits himself the wild radicalism of woman suffrage. But as regards vested interests and patriotism and war he is a conservative, practically a troglodyte. What he attacks with fervor are the delinquents in ordinary conduct, especially the people who lack self-control. " Booze-hoisters " and card-players and tango-dancers and cigarette-smokers are his pet abominations — genuine abominations. Profanity, strange to say, is another evil that he fights with fire. Honesty, sobriety, chastity — these are virtues that he exalts, illustrating the horror of failing in them by means of innumerable chromatic anecdotes. The devil he constantly attacks, though never with real solemnity. " The devil has been practicing for six thousand years and he has never had appendicitis, rheumatism or tonsilitis. If you get to playing tag with the devil he will beat you every chip." It is more for spice and snap that he introduces the devil than to terrify his public. The Bible is his serious theme, and he feels about it almost the way Martin Tupper did:

> The dear old Family Bible should be still our champion volume,
> The Medo-Persic law to us, the standard of our Rights . . .
> It is a joy, an honor, yea a wisdom, to declare
> A boundless, an infantile faith in our dear English Bible!
> The garden, and the apple, and the serpent, and the ark,
> And every word in every verse, and in its literal meaning,
> And histories and prophecies and miracles and visions,
> In spite of learned unbelief,— we hold it all plain truth:
> Not blindly, but intelligently, after search and study;
> Hobbes and Paine considered well, and Germany and Colenso . . .
> The Bible made us what we are, the mightiest Christian nation . . .
> The Bible, standing in its strength a pyramid four-square,
> The plain old English Bible, a gem with all its flaws . . .
> Is still the heaven-blest fountain of conversion and salvation.

One of Billy Sunday's boasts is that the liquor interests hate him. " That dirty, stinking bunch of moral assassins hires men to sit in the audience to hear me, to write down what I say and then try to find some author who said something like it, and accuse me of having stolen my ideas. I know that $30,000 was offered a man in New York City to write a series of articles attacking me. All right; if you know anything about me that you want to publish, go to it. Everything they say about me is a dirty, stinking, black-hearted lie. The whole thing is a frame-up from A to Izzard. I'll fight them till hell freezes over, and then borrow a pair of skates. By the grace of God, I've helped to make Colorado and Nebraska and Iowa and Michigan and West Virginia dry, and I serve notice on the dirty gang that I'll help to make the whole nation dry." (New York Times, April 19th, 1917.)

Assuming these points to be well taken, there is still great room to doubt the deep religious effect of a Billy Sunday revival. Men like William Allen White and Henry Allen have testified on his behalf in Kansas, and he has the undying gratitude of many hundred human beings for moral stimulus in a time of need. In spite of the thousands who have hit the sawdust trail, however, it is difficult to believe that more than a tiny proportion of his auditors are religiously affected by him. The great majority of those who hit the trail are people who merely want to shake his hand. Very few give any signs of seriousness or " conversion." The atmosphere of the tabernacle, bright with electric light and friendly with hymn-singing, is not religiously inspiring, and in the voice and manner of Billy Sunday there is seldom a contagious note. His audiences are curi-

ous to see him and hear him. He is a remarkable
public entertainer, and much that he says has keen
humor and verbal art and horse sense. But for all
his militancy, for all his pugnacious vociferation, he
leaves an impression of being at once violent and
incommunicative, a sales agent for Christianity but
not a guide or a friend.

Still, as between Billy Sunday's gymnastics and
the average oyster soup, Messrs. Wanamaker and
Rockefeller naturally put their money on Sunday.
Theirs is the world of business enterprise, of car-
pets and socks, Socony and Nujol, and if Christ
could have been put over in the same way, by live-
wire salesmanship, Billy was the man.

FIFTH AVENUE AND FORTY-SECOND STREET

I

"THOUGH you do not know it, I have a soul.
Behold, across the way, my library. When the
night shrouds those lions and the fresh young trees
shake out their greenery against the white stone-
work, do you not catch a suggestion of atmosphere,
something of a mood? And the black cliffs around,
with the janitress lights making jeweled bars the
width of them, are they not monuments? I cleave
brilliantly, up and down this dormant city. It is
for you, late wayfarer. Pay no heed to the plod-
ding milk-wagon or the hatless young maiden speeding her lover's motor. Heed my long silences, my
slim tall darknesses. My human tide has ebbed.
My buildings come about me to muse and to com-
mune. Receive, for once on Fifth Avenue, the soul
that is imprisoned in my stone and steel."

It is not for the respectable, this polite communication. Theatre and club and restaurant have
long since disgorged these. New York has masti-
cated their money. They have done as they should
and are restored uptown. Even the old news-
woman, she who had spent starving months in the
Russian woods, caught in the first eddies of the war,
she has tottered from her stand down by the station.
The Hungarian waiter in Childs' is still there, still

assuaging the deep nocturnal need for buckwheat cakes, but that is off the avenue. It is three, the avenue is nearly empty. It is ready to disclose its soul.

But before this subtle performance there is a preliminary. It is a very self-respecting avenue and at three on a pleasant morning, when no one is around to disturb it, it proceeds to take its bath. Perhaps a few motors go by — a taxi rolling north, heavy with night thoughts, a tired white face framed in its black depth; or a Wanamaker truck clanking loosely home in the other direction, delivered of its suburban chores. The Italian acolytes are impartial. They spray the wheels of a touring car with gusto, ignored by its linked lovers, or drive a powerful stream under the hubs of a Nassau News wagon trundling to a train. The avenue must be refreshed, the brave green of the library trees nodding approval, the sparrows expecting it. It must be prepared for the sun, under bold lamps and timid stars.

A fine young morning, the watchman promises. A bit of wind whiffles the water that is shot out from the white-wing's hose, but it is clearing up above and looks well for the day. The hour beckons memories for the watchman — fine young mornings he used to have long ago, in Ireland, a boy on his first adventure and he driving with the barley to Ross.

It is an empty street. The hose is wheeled away over the glistening asphalt. The watchman disappears — he has a cozy nook beyond the ken of time-clocks. The last human pigmy seeks his pillow, to hide a diminished head. With man ac-

[33]

counted for, night sighs its completion and creeps to the west. Then, untrammeled of heaven or minion, the buildings have their moment. Each tower stretches his proud height to the morning. The stones give out their spirit; their music is unsealed.

II

Fifth Avenue stands serene and still, but it cannot hold the virgin morning forever. Its windows may be blank, its sidewalks vacant. Behind the walls there is a magnet drawing back its human life.

"Give us this day our daily bread." A saintly venerable horse seems to know the injunction. Emerging from nowhere, ambling to nowhere, it usurps the innocent morning in answer to the Lord.

And not by bread alone. There is nothing in the prayer about clams, but some one in Mount Vernon is destined to have them quickly. Out of the mysterious south, racing against time, a little motor flits onward with gaping barrels of clams. At a decent interval comes a heavier load of fish. Great express wagons follow, commissarial giants. The honest uses of Fifth Avenue begin.

Butchers and bakers are out before fine ladies. The grocer and the greengrocer are early on their rounds. But an empty American News truck confesses that eternal vigilance is the price of circulation. Its gait is swifter than the gait of milkman or fruit-and-vegetable man. Dust and dew are on the florist's wheels: he has come whistling by the swamps of Flushing. His flimsy automobile runs lightly past the juggernauts that crush down.

Uncle Sam is in haste at six in the morning. His trucks hurl from Grand Central to make the sub-stations. But his is not the pride of place. Nor is it coal or farmers' feed that appropriates the middle of the street. The noblest wagons, a long parade of them, announce the greater glory of beer. The temperance advocate may shudder at the desecration of the morning. He may observe "Hell Gate Brewery" and nod his sickly nod. But there is something about this large preparedness for thirst that stills the carping worm of conscience. It is good to see what solid, ample caravans are required to replenish man with beer. It is not the single glass that is glorious. It is not even the single car-load. It is the steady, deliberate, ponderous procession that streams through the early hours. Once it seemed as if Percherons alone were worthy of beer-wagons. It satisfied the faith that there was Design in creation, but the Percheron is not needed. There is the same institutional impressiveness about a motor-truck piled to the sky with beer.

III

"Number, please?" She is anonymous, that inquirer. But behind her anonymity there is humanity. Fifth Avenue and Forty-second Street caught a glimpse of her at six forty-five A. M.

She was up at five in the morning. She had a pang as she put on her check suit, slightly darker than her check coat lined with pink. Her little hat, however, was smart and new. Her mother cooked breakfast while she set the table. Then she walked to the Third Avenue " L " with her friend. They got off the express at Forty-second Street, rode to Fourth Avenue on the short spur line, and walked along Forty-second Street in time for them to do a brief window-shopping as they passed the shirt-waists at Forsythe's. Her friend's bronze shoes she envied as they crossed the little park back of the Library. On Sixth Avenue they inspected the window at Bernstein's. A slight argument engrossed them. They hovered over the window, chirping not unlike the sparrows in Bryant Park. Then, in a flurry of punctuality, they raced for the telephone company to begin their " Number, please."

An hour earlier laborers with dinner-pails had crossed Fifth Avenue, and hatless Polish girls on their way to scrub. By seven o'clock the negro porters and laborers were giving way to white-collar strap-hangers on the elevateds and in the subway. It was getting to be the hour of salesmen and sales-girls and office-boys and shop-subordinates and clerks. The girls back of the scenes at the mil-liner's, they go up Fifth Avenue at seven, to take one side-street or another. The girl who sells you a toothbrush in the drug-store hurries by the shop windows, herself as neat as a model. Is it early? Myriads of men are pouring down already. Be-sides, " 'S use of kickin' ? If you don't like it, you can walk out ! "

The night-watchman is going home, and an old at-tendant from the Grand Central. " Tired, Pop? " " Yeh, p'tty tired." " What right 've you to git tired workin' for a big corporation? " The op-pressed wage-slave bellows, " Ha, ha."

IV

Of these things Fifth Avenue is innocent at five in the afternoon. The diastole of travelers had spread all morning from Grand Central; the systole is active at five. As the great muscle contracts in the afternoon, atoms are pulled frantically to the suburbs, tearing their way through the weaker streams that are drawn up by the neighboring shops and clubs and bars and hotels. The Biltmore and Sherry's and Delmonico's and the Manhattan and the Belmont are no longer columnar monuments, holding secret vigil. They are secondary to the human floods which they suck in and spray out. The street itself is lost to memory and vision. A swollen stream, dammed at moments while chosen people are permitted to walk dry-shod across, bears on its restless bosom the freight of curiosity and pride and favor. One might fancy, to gaze on this mad throng of motors, that a new religious sect had conquered the universe, worshipers of a machine.

It is the hour of white gloves and delicate profiles, the feminine hour. A little later there will be more leaves than blossoms, the men coming from work giving a duller tone. But one is permitted to believe for this period that Fifth Avenue has a personality, parti-colored, decorative, flashing, frivolous, composed of many styles and many types. The working world intersects it rudely at Forty-second Street, but scarcely infiltrates it. A qualification distinguishes those who turn up and down the Avenue. It is not leisure that distinguishes them, or money, but their sense that there is romance in the appearance of money and leisure. Many of the white gloves are cotton. Many of the gloves are not white. But it is May-time, the afternoon, Fifth Avenue. One may pretend the world is gay.

They seem chaotic and impulsive, these crowds on Fifth Avenue. They move as by personal will. But dawn and sunset, morning and evening, common attractions govern them. There is a rhythm in these human tides.

V

For eighty years Henri Fabre watched the insects. He stayed with his friend the spider the round of the clock. Time, that reveals the spider, is also eloquent of man in his city. Time is the scene-shifter and the detective. Some day we should pitch a metropolitan observatory at the corner of Fifth Avenue and Forty-second Street,— some day, if we can find the time.

AS AN ALIEN FEELS

TWENTY-FIVE years ago I knew but dimly that the United States existed. My first dream of it came, as well as I remember, from the strange gay flag that blew above a circus tent on the Fair Green. It was a Wild West Show, and for years I associated America with the intoxication of the circus and, for no reason, with the tang of oranges. " Two a penny, two a penny, large penny oranges! Buy away an' ate away, large penny oranges! " They were oranges from Seville then, but the odor of them and the fumes of circus excitement gave me a first gay ribald sense of the United States.

The next allied sense was gathered from a scallawag uncle. He had sought his fortune in America — sought it, as I infer now, on the rear end of a horse-car. When he came home he was full of odd and delicious oaths. " Gosh hell hang it " was his chief touch of American culture. He was a " Yank " in local parlance, a frequently drunken Yank. His fine drooping mustache too often drooped with porter. Once, a boy of nine, I steadied him home under the October stars and absorbed a long alcoholic reverie on the Horseshoe Falls. As we slept together that night in the rat-pattering loft, and as he absently appropriated all the horse-blanket, I had plenty of chance to shiver over the wonderments of the Horseshoe Falls.

This, with an instilled idea that America and

America alone could offer "work," foreshadowed the American landscape. It is the bald hope of work that finally magnetizes us hither. But every dream and every loyalty was with the unhappy land from which I came.

For many months the music of New York harbor spoke only of home. Every outgoing steamer that opened its throat made me homesick. America was New York, and New York was down town, and down town was a vortex of new duties. There I learned the bewildering foreign tongue of earning a living, and the art of eating at Childs'. At night the hall-bedroom near Broadway, and the resourceless promenade up and down Broadway for amusement. The only women to say "dear," the women who say it on the street.

In Chicago, not in New York, I found the United States. The word "settlement" gave me my first puzzled intimation that there was somewhere a clew to this grim struggle down town. I had looked for it in boarding-houses. I had looked for it in stenographic night-schools. I had sought it in the blotchy Sunday newspaper, in Coney Island, in long jaunts up the Palisades. I had looked for it among the street-walkers, the first to proffer intimacy. And of course, not being clever enough, I had overlooked it. But in Chicago, as I say, I came on it at home.

America dawned for me in a social settlement. It dawned for me as a civilization and a faith. In all my first experiences of my employers I got not one glimpse of American civilization. Theirs was the language of smartness, alertness, brightness, success, efficiency, and I tried to learn it, but it was a

difficult and alien tongue. Some of them were law-
yers, but they were interested in penmanship and
ability to clean ink-bottles. Some of them were
business men, but they were interested in ability to
typewrite and to keep the petty cash. It was not
their fault. Ours was not an affair of the heart.
But if it had not been for the social settlement, I
should still be an alien to the bone.

Till I knew a social settlement the American flag
was still a flag on a circus-tent, a gay flag but cheap.
The cheapness of the United States was the message of quick-lunch and the boarding-house, of vaudeville and Coney Island and the Sunday newspaper,
of the promenade on Broadway. In the social settlement I came on something entirely different.
Here on the ash-heap of Chicago was a blossom of
something besides success. The house was saturated
in the perfume of the stockyards, to make it sweet.
A trolley-line ran by its bedroom windows, to make
it musical. It was thronged with Jews and Greeks
and Italians and soulful visitors, to make it restful.
It was inhabited by highstrung residents, to make it
easy. But it was the first place in all America
where there came to me a sense of the intention of
democracy, the first place where I found a flame
by which the melting-pot melts. I heard queer
words about it. The men, I learned, were molly-
coddles, and the women were sexually unemployed.
The ruling class spoke of " unsettlement workers "
with animosity, the socialists of a mealy-mouthed
compromise. Yet in that strange haven of clear
humanitarian faith I discovered what I suppose I
had been seeking—the knowledge that America had
a soul.

How one discovers these things it is hard to put honestly. It is like trying to recall the first fair wind of spring. But I know that slowly and unconsciously the atmosphere of the settlement thawed out the asperity of alienism. There were Americans of many kinds in residence, from Illinois, from Michigan, from New York, English-Americans, Russian-Americans, Austrian-Americans, German-Americans, men who had gone to Princeton and Harvard, women spiritually lavendered in Bryn Mawr. The place bristled with hyphens. But the Americanism was of a kind that opened to the least pressure from without, and never shall I forget the way these residents with their " North Side " friends had managed so graciously to domesticate the annual festival of my own nationality. That, strange though it may seem, is the more real sort of Americanization Day.

From Walt Whitman, eventually, the naturalizing alien breathes in American air, but I doubt if I should have ever known the meaning of Walt Whitman had I not lived in that initiating home. It was easy in later years to see new meanings in the American flag, to stand with Ethiopia Saluting the Colors, but it was in the settlement I found the sources from which it was dyed. For there, to my amazement, one was not expected to believe that man's proper place is on a Procrustean bed of profiteering. A different tradition of America lived there, one in which the earlier faiths had come through, in which the way to heaven was not necessarily up a skyscraper. In New England, later, I found many ideas of which the settlement was symptomatic, but as I imbibed them they were " America " for me.

[42]

What it means to come at last into possession of Lincoln, whose spirit is so precious to the social settlement, is probably unintelligible to Lincoln's normal inheritors. To understand this, however, is to understand the birth of a loyalty. In the countries from which we come there have been men of such humane ideals, but they have almost without exception been men beyond the pale. The heroes of the peoples of Europe have not been the governors of Europe. They have been the spokesmen of the governed. But here among America's governors and statesmen was a simple authenticator of humane ideals. To inherit him becomes for the European not an abandonment of old loyalties, but a summary of them in a new. In the microcosm of the settlement perhaps Lincolnism is too simple. Many of one's promptest acquiescences are revised as one meets and eats with the ruling class later on. But the salt of this American soil is Lincoln. When one finds that, one is naturalized.

It is curious how the progress of naturalization becomes revealed to one. I still recollect with a thrill the first time I attended a national political convention and listened to the roll-call of the States. "Alabama! Arizona! Arkansas!" Empty names for many years, at last they were filled with one clear concept, the concept of the democratic experiment. "As I have walk'd in Alabama my morning walk"— the living appeal to each state by name recalled Whitman's generous amusing scope. "Far breath'd land! Arctic braced! Mexican breez'd! The diverse! The compact! The Pennsylvanian! The Virginian! The double Carolinian!" The orotund roll-call was not intended to evoke Whitman. It was intended, as it happened, to evoke votes for Taft and Sherman. But even these men were parts of the democratic experiment. And the vastly peopled hall answered for Walt Whitman, as the empurpled Penrose did not answer. It was they who were the leaves of our grass.

In Whitman, as William James has shown, there is an arrant mysticism which his own Democratic Vistas exposed in cold light. Yet into this credulity as to the virtue and possibilities of the people an alien is likely to enter if his first intimacy with America came in the aliens' crêche. A settlement is a crêche for the step-children of Europe, and it is hard not to credit America at large with some of the impulses which make the settlement. Such, at any rate, is the tendency I experienced myself.

With this tendency, what of loyalty to the United States? I think of Lincoln and his effected mysticism by Union, union for the experiment, and I feel alive within me a complete identification with this land. The keenest realization of the nation reached me, as I recall, the first time I saw the capitol in Washington. Quite unsuspecting I strolled up the hill from the station, just about midnight, the streets gleaming after a warm shower. The plaza in front of the capitol was deserted. A few high sentinel lamps threw a lonely light down the wet steps and scantily illumined the pillars. Darkness veiled the dome. Standing apart completely by myself, I felt as never before the union of which this strength and simplicity was the symbol. The quietude of the night, the scent of April pervading it, gave to the lonely building a dignity such as I had seldom felt before. It seemed to me to stand for a fine and achieved determination, for a purpose maintained, for a quiet faith in the peoples and states that lay away behind it to far horizons. Lincoln, I thought, had perhaps looked from those steps on such a night in April, and felt the same promise of spring.

SCIENTIFIC MANAGEMENT

ONE should not be ashamed to acknowledge the pursuit of the secret of life. That secret, however, is shockingly elusive. It is quite visible to me, somewhere in space. Like a ball swung before a kitten, it taunts my eye. Like a kitten I cannot help making a lunge after it. But tied to the ball there seems to be a mischievous invisible string. My eye fixes the secret of life but it escapes my paw.

During the Russo-Japanese War I thought I had it. It involved a great deal of stern discipline. Physically it meant giving up meat, Boston garters and cigarettes. It seemed largely composed of rice, hot baths followed by rolling in the snow and jiu jitsu. The art of jiu jitsu hinted at the very secret itself. Here was the crude West seeking to slug its way to mastery while the commonest Japanese had only to lay hold of life by the little finger to reduce it to squealing submission. The sinister power of jiu jitsu haunted me. Unless the West could learn it we were putty in Japanese hands. It was the acme of effortless subtlety. A people with such an art, combined with ennobling vegetarianism, must necessarily be a superior people. I privately believed that the Japanese had employed it in sinking the Russian fleet.

Thomas Alva Edison displaced jiu jitsu in my soul and supplanted it with a colossal contempt for sleep. An insincere contempt for food I already protested. No nation could hope to take the field that subsisted on heavy foods — such unclean things as sausages and beer. The secret of world mastery was a diet of rice. "We all eat too much" became a fixed conviction. But Mr. Edison forced a greater conviction — we all sleep too much as well. This thought had first come to me from Arnold Bennett. Sleep was a matter of habit, of bad habit. We sleep ourselves stupid. Who could not afford to lose a minute's sleep? Reduce sleep by a minute a day — who would miss it? And in 500 days you would have got down to the classical forty winks. Mr. Edison did not merely preach this gospel. He modestly indicated his own career to illustrate its successful practicability. To cut down sleep and cut down food was the only way to function like a super-man.

Once started on this question of habits I spent a life of increasing turmoil. From Plato I heard the word moderation, but from William Blake I learned that "the road of excess leads to the palace of wisdom." From Benjamin Franklin I gathered the importance of good habits, but William James glee-fully told me to avoid all habits, even good ones. And then came Scientific Management.

The concept of scientific management practically wrecked my life. I discovered that there was a right way of doing everything and that I was doing everything wrongly. It was no new idea to me that we were all astray about the simplest things. We did not know how to breathe properly. We did not know how to sit properly. We did not know how to walk properly. We wore a hard hat: it was

making us bald.   We wore pointed shoes: it was un-
fair to our little toe.   But scientific management did
not   dawdle   over   such   details.   It   nonchalantly
pointed   out   that   " waste   motions "   were   the   chief
characteristic of our lives.

One of the most fantastic persons in the world is
the public official who, before he can write a postal
order or a tax receipt, has to make preliminary curls
of penmanship in the air.   Observed by the scientific
eye, we are much more fantastic ourselves.   If our
effective motions could be registered on a visual tar-
get, our record would be found to resemble that of
savages who use ammunition without a sight on their
guns.   If we think that the ordinary soldier's marks-
manship is wasteful, we may well look to ourselves.
Our life is peppered with motions that fly wide and
wild.   It begins on awaking.   We stretch our arms
— waste motion!   We ought to utilize that gesture for polishing our shoes.   We rub our eyes —
more foolishness.   We should rub our eyes on Sunday for the rest of the week.   But it is in processes
like shaving that scientific management is really
needed.   Men flatter themselves that they shave
with the minimum of gesture.   They believe that
they complete the operation under five minutes.
But, excusing their inaccuracy, do they know that
under the inspection of the scientific manager their
performance would look as jagged as their razor-
blade under the microscope?   The day will probably
arrive when a superman will shave with one superb
motion, as delightful to the soul as the uncoiling of
an orange-skin in one long unbroken peel.

In reading the newspaper a man most betrays the
haphazard, unscrutinized conduct of his morn.   We

pick up our paper without any suspicion that we are about to commit intellectual felony. We do not know that the news editor is in a conspiracy to play on our minds. If men gyrate too much physically, they certainly are just as anarchistic when they start to look over the news. It is not so much that they begin the day with devouring the details of a murder or lull themselves with some excuse for not reading a British note on the blockade. It is the fact that they are led by a ring running through their instincts to obey the particular editors they read.

Viewing myself as a human machine, I cannot understand how the human race has survived. Even conceding that I was normal, it is so much the worse for normality. I simply belong to a monstrous breed. There is not one important layman's practice that we have organized with regard to discipline and efficiency. If bricklayers waste motions in laying bricks, how about the motions wasted in lifting one's hat and the circumvolutions in putting links in one's cuffs? How about the impulsive child who wastes motions so recklessly in giving his mother a hug? The discovery seemed chilly that everything could be scientifically managed, everything could be perfected if one took up an altitudinous position at the center of one's life. But a fear of being chilly is a mark of inferiority. It ill becomes a human machine.

Yearning to live scrupulously on twenty-four hours a day, with vague longings to eat very little and sleep very little and master jiu jitsu and breathe deep and chew hard and practice Mueller exercises and give up tobacco and coffee and hug my mother scientifically and save waste motions in putting on my shirt, I happened to come across two European thinkers, a physician and a metaphysician. Paralleling Shakespeare's knowledge of dead languages by my own knowledge of live ones, I could not read these masters in the original to determine whether they blended like oil and vinegar or fought like water and oil. But in the eagerness of philosophic poverty I grasped just two delightful words from them, "instinct" and "repression." The metaphysician's secret of life, apparently, was to drop using one's so-called intelligence so frantically, to become more like those marvels of instinct, the hyena and the whale. The physician merely seemed to put the Ten Commandments in their place. To tell the truth, his detection of "repression" gave me no tangible promise. I exculpate the doctor. But the evolutionist turned my thoughts away from the early worries of discipline. This is the latest ball in the air that the kitten is chasing, with no suspicion of any tantalizing invisible string.

THE NEXT NEW YORK

YOU'D get awfully tired if I told you everything about my visit to New York in A. D. 1991. Some things are too complicated even to refer to, many things I've already forgotten, and a number of things I didn't understand. But as I had to return to my work as prison doctor in 1919 after a week of 1991 I grasped a few top impressions that may interest you. I hope I can give them to you straight.

The people on the street took my eye the minute I arrived in town. They looked so pleasing and they wore such stunning clothes. You know that at present, with the long indoor working day and the mixture of embalmed and storage and badly cooked food, the number of pasty-faced and emaciated men and women is very high. I exempt the hearty sweating classes like the structural iron workers and teamsters and porters and even policemen. You could recruit a fine-looking club from the building trades. But stand any afternoon on Fifth Avenue and size up the condition of the passers-by. You see shopgirls in thin cotton who are under-weight, under-slept, miserably nourished and devitalized. You see pimply waiters and stooping clerks. You see weary, fish-eyed mothers who look as if every day was washing day. Scores of sagging middle-aged people go by, who ought to be taken to a clinic. A little earlier in the afternoon it's almost impossible to share the sidewalk with the squat factory hands who overflow at the lunch hour. They're hard to kill, these poor fellows, but they're a puny, stinking, stunted, ill-favored horde. But the greater cleanliness of the people later on, and their better clothes, doesn't put them in a very different class. You hear a good deal about the queens you see, but, really, the city streets of New York in 1919, streaming with people who have dun clothes to match dun faces, make you wonder what's the use.

These people in 1991 were good to look at! The three-hour working day had a lot to do with it, of course, and the basic economic changes. But what leads me first to speak of appearances is the huge responsibility that had gone to hygienists. I mean educational and administrative. In 1991, I found, people were really acting on the theory that you can't have civilization without sound bodies. The idea itself was as old as an old joke, a platitude in the mouth of every pill-vender. But the city was working on it as if it were a pivotal truth, and this meant a total revision of ordinary conduct.

Building the Panama Canal was a simple little job compared to making New York hygienic. Thirty years must have been spent in getting the folks to realize that no man and woman had any hygienic excuse for breeding children within the city limits. It was sixty years, I was told, before it was official that a city child was an illegitimate child. At first mothers kicked hard when the illegitimates were confiscated, but in the end they came to see justice in the human version of the slogan, " an acre and a cow." It got rid of the good old city-bred medical formula that the best way to handle pregnancy is to handle it as a pathological condition. Of course this prohibition movement made all sorts of people mad. A bunch of Gold Coast women held out for a long time on the score of personal liberty. Women had private city babies where the inspectors couldn't get at them. You know, just like private whisky. But in the end the prohibitionists won, and it had an enormous effect on cleaning up Manhattan. It cut out all but the detached and the transient residents, and with the breathing space rules, these were far less than you'd suppose. Even with the great area of garden-roofs, the fixed residents were not much more than 100,000.

This demobilization wasn't special to New York. In other places there were much more rigid " units." Hygiene, nothing else, decided the unit size of cities in 1991. The old sprawling haphazard heterogeneous city gave place to the " modern " unit, permanent residences within the city never being open to families that had children under fourteen. For the heads of such families, however, the transportation problem was beautifully solved. Every unit city came to be so constructed that within half an hour of the " fresh air and exercise " homes, men and women could reach factories and warehouses in one direction, and offices and courts and banks and exchanges in another. This was after they realized the high cost of noise and dirt. The noiseless, dirtless, swift, freight train took the place of most trucks, and of course the remaining trucks shot up and down the non-pedestrian sanitary alleys. Another thing that interested me was the plexus of all the things that are to be exhibited. This involved a great problem for New York before factories were

deported and the moving " H. G. Wells " sidewalks
introduced. How to economize time and space, and
yet not produce too close a homogeneity, too protein
an intellectual and æsthetic and social diet, became
a fascinating question. But the devotion of Blackwell's Island to summer and winter art and music,
with all the other islands utilized for permanent exhibitions gave the city directors a certain leeway.
The islands were made charming. I was quite
struck over there, I think, on a new island in Flushing Bay, by the guild-managed shows of clothing,
where you sat and watched the exhibits traveling on
an endless belt, that stopped when you wanted it to
— the kind that art exhibitions adopted for certain
purposes. You see, the old department stores had
passed away as utterly as the delivery horse and
display advertising and the non-preventive physician.
And the old game of " seasons " and fashions was
abandoned soon after the celebrated trial of Condé
Nast for the undermining of the taste of shopgirls.
The job of the purchasing consumer was steadily
simplified. Youth of both sexes learned fairly early
in life what they could and what they couldn't do
personally in the use of color. No one thought of
copying another's color or design in dress any more
than of copying another's oculist prescription. And
with the guild consultants always ready to help out
the troubled buyer, the business of shopping for
clothes became as exciting and intelligent as the pas-
time of visiting a private exhibition. In this way,
backed up by the guilds, a daring employment of
color became generally favored. But a big item in
this programme was the refusal of the guilds to pre-
scribe any costumes for people who needed medical

[54]

care first.   It was useless, the guilds said, to deco-
rate a mud-pie.   And the hygienists agreed.

So you got back always to the doctrine of a sound
body.   In the hygienic riots of 1936 some horrible
lynchings took place.   An expert from the Chicago
stockyards was then running the New York subways.
He devised the upper-berth system by which the
space between people's heads and the roof of the
car could be used on express trains for hanging up
passengers, like slabs of bacon.   It was only after a
few thousand citizens had failed to respond to the
pulmotor which was kept at every station to revive
weaklings, that the divine right of human beings to
decent transportation became a real public issue.
The hygienists made the great popular mistake of
trying to save the stockyards man.   They knew he
had a sick soul.   They believed that by psycho-
analyzing him and showing he had always wanted to
skin cats alive, they could put the traction question
on a higher plane.   Unfortunately the Hearst of
that era took up the issue on the so-called popular
side.   He denounced the hygienists as heartless experts and showed how science was really a conspiracy
in favor of the ruling class.   The hygienic riots re-
sulted in a miserable set-back to the compulsory
psycho-analysis of all criminals, but the bloody assas-
sination of the leading hygienist of the day brought
about a reaction, and within thirty years no judge
was allowed to serve who wasn't an expert in psychic
work and hygiene.   This decision was greatly aided
by the publication of a brochure revealing the relation of criminal verdicts to the established neuroses
of city magistrates.   The promise that this work
would be extended and published as a supplement to

the Federal Reporter went a long way toward converting the Bar. The old pretensions of the Bar went rapidly to pieces when political use was made of important psychological and physiological facts. The hygienists spoke of " the mighty stream of morbid compulsion broadening down to more morbid compulsion." By 1950 no man with an Œdipus complex could even get on the Real Estate ticket, and the utter collapse of militarism came about with the magnificently scientific biographies of all the prominent armament advocates in the evil era.

I had a surprise coming for me in the total disappearance of prisons. Though I hate to confess it, I was a little amazed when I found that the old penology was just as historical in 1991 as the methodology of the Spanish Inquisition. Scientific men did possess models of prisons like Sing Sing and Trenton and Atlanta and Leavenworth, and the tiny advances in the latter prisons were thought amusing. But the deformity of the human minds and the social systems that permitted such prisons as ours was a matter for acute discussion and analysis everywhere, even in casual unspecialized groups. This general intelligence made it clear to me that social hygiene was never understood up to the middle of the twentieth century. The very name, after all, was appropriated by men afraid to specify the sex diseases they were then cleaning up. Puritanism, serviceable as it was in its time, had kept men from obtaining and examining the evidence necessary to right conclusions about conduct. " Think," said one delightful youth to me, on my first day in 1991, " think of not knowing the first facts as to the physiological laws of continence. Think of starting out after general physical well-being by the preposterous road of universal military service. Think of electing Congressmen in the old days without applying even the Binet test to them. Why, to-day we know nothing about ' the pursuit of happiness,' fair as that object is, and yet we should no more stand for such indiscriminateness than we'd allow a day to go by without swimming."

The youth, I should specify, was a female youth, what we call a girl. I had nothing to say to her. But my mind shot back to 1919, to which I was so soon to return, and I thought of a millionaire's device I had once seen in Chicago. Deep in the basement of a great factory building there was a small electric-lighted cell, and in this bare cell there was a gymnastic framework, perhaps four feet high, on which was strapped an ordinary leather saddle. In front of the saddle there rose two thin steel sticks, and out of them came thin leather reins. By means of a clever arrangement of springs down below that responded to an electric current, the whole mechanism was able to move up and down and backward and forward in short stabby jerks that were supposed to stir up your gizzard in practically the same way as the motion of a horse. This was, in fact, a synthetic horse, bearing the same æsthetic relation to a real horse that a phonograph song does to a real song that is poured out, so to speak, in the sun. And here, in the bald basement cell with its two barred basement windows (closed), the constipated millionaires take their turns, whenever they can bear it, going through the canned motions of a ride, staring with bored eyes at the blind tiled wall in front of them. So far, in 1919, had the worship of

[57]

Hygeia carried the helot-captains of industry. And from that basement, from that heathen symbol of perverted exercise, men had returned to a primary acceptance of the human body and a primary law that its necessities be everywhere observed. Not such a great accomplishment, I thought, in seventy years. And yet it gave to mankind the leg-up they had to have for the happiness they long for.

CHICAGO

A GOOD deal of nonsense is talked about the personality of towns. What most people enjoy about a town is familiarity, not personality, and they can give no penetrating account of their affection. "What is the finest town in the world?" the New York reporters recently asked a young recruit, eager for him to eulogize New York. "Why," he answered, "San Malo, France. I was born there." That is the usual reason, perhaps the best reason, why a person likes any place on earth. The clew is autobiographical.

But towns do have personality. Contrast London and New York, or Portland and Norfolk, or Madison and St. Augustine. Chicago certainly has a personality, and it would be obscurantism of the most modern kind to pretend that there was no " soul " in Chicago either to like or to dislike. People who have never lived in Chicago are usually content with disliking it, and those who have seen it superficially, or smelled it in passing when the stockyard factories were making glue, can seldom understand why Chicagoans love it. Official visitors, of course, profess to admire it, with the eagerness of anxious missionaries seeking to make good with cannibals. But except for men who knew Bursley or

Chicago, by H. C. Chatfield-Taylor. Illustrations by Lester G. Hornby. Boston: Houghton Mifflin Co.

Belfast, and slipped into Chicago as into old slippers — men like Arnold Bennett and George Bermingham — there are few outsiders who really feel at home. Stevenson passed through it on his immigrant journey across the plains, pondering that one who had so promptly subscribed a sixpence to restore the city after the fire should be compelled to pay for his own ham and eggs. He thought Chicago great but gloomy. Kipling shrank from it like a sensitive plant. It horrified him. H. G. Wells thought it amazing, but chiefly amazing as a lapse from civilization. All of these leave little doubt how Chicago first hits the eye. It is, in fact, dirty, unruly and mean. It has size without spaciousness, opportunity without imaginativeness, action without climax, wealth without distinction. A sympathetic artist finds picturesqueness in it, though far from gracious where most characteristic; but for the most part it is shoddy, dingy and vulgar, making more noise downtown than a boiler works, and raining smuts all day as a symbolic reproach from heaven. It is not for its beaux yeux that the outsider begins to love the town.

But a great town is like the elephant of the fable; one must see it altogether before one can define it; one can believe almost anything monstrous from a partial view. Time, in the case of Chicago, is supremely necessary — about three years as a minimum. Then its goodness passeth all pre-matrimonial understanding; its essence is disclosed.

Mr. H. C. Chatfield-Taylor has qualified, so far as time is concerned, to speak of Chicago, and I think it would be churlish not to agree that from the standpoint of the old settler he has done his city proud. All old Chicagoans will recognize at once why Mr. Taylor should go back to the beginning, and they will be delighted at the clarity with which the early history is expounded, as well as the era before the Civil War. They will also understand and rejoice over the repetition of grand old names — Gordon S. Hubbard, John Kinzie, Mark Beaubien, Uranus H. Crosby, Sherman of the Sherman hotel, General Hart L. Stewart and Long John Wentworth. In every town in the world there is, of course, a Long John or a Big Bill, but Chicagoans will savor this reference to their own familiar, and will delight in the snug feeling that they too " knew Chicago when." Mr. Taylor is also dear to his townsmen when he harks back to days before the Fire. In those days the West-siders were a little superior because they had the Episcopal Cathedral of Saints Peter and Paul, and the church-going folk could hear the " fast young men " speeding trotting horses past the church doors. Such performances seemed fairly worldly, but later did not Mr. Taylor himself drive his high-steppers to the races at Washington Park, and did he not woo the heart of the city where gilded youth cherished a " nod of recognition from Potter Palmer, John B. Drake, or John A. Rice." The dinners of antelope steak and roast buffalo at the Grand Pacific recall a Chicago antedating the World's Fair that left strong traces into the twentieth century, a Chicago that is commemorated with grace and kindliness in the fair pages of this book.

But this is not enough. If Mr. Taylor's heart lingers among the " marble-fronts " of his youth, this is not peculiarly Chicagoan. Such fond reminiscence is the common nature of man. And a better basis for loving Chicago must be offered than the evidence that one teethed on it, battered darling that it is. Mr. Taylor's better explanation, as I read it, is extremely significant. He identifies himself fully and eagerly with the New Englanders who made the town. Bounty-jumpers and squatters and speculators, war widows and politicians and anarchists and aliens — all these go into his perspective, as do the emergencies of the Fire and the splendors of the Fair. But the marrow of his pride in Chicago is his community with its origins in " men, like myself, of New England blood, whose fathers felled our forests and tilled our prairie land." Since the time he was born, he tells us, more than two million people have been added to the population of Chicago. Only a fifth of the Great West Side are now American-born, and the Lake Shore Drive was still a cemetery when Mr. Taylor was a boy on that dignified West Side. This links Mr. Taylor closely to the beginning of things. Hence he likes to insist in his kindly spirit that Chicago's puritan " aristocracy " is the source of Chicago altruism, that " the society of Chicago [is] more puritanical than that of any great city in the world," and that " back of Chicago's strenuousness and vim stands the spirit of her founders holding her in leash, the tenets of the Pilgrim Fathers being still a potent factor in her life . . . She possesses a New England conscience to leaven her diverse character and make her truly — the pulse of America."

Every bird takes what he finds to build his own spiritual nest. Personally, I love Chicago, ugly and wild and rude, but I prefer to see it as an impuritan.

Its sprawling hideousness, indeed, has always seemed a direct result of the private-minded policy that distinguished Chicago's big little men. The triumvirate that Mr. Taylor mentions had no statesmanship in them. One was an admirable huckster, another an inflexible paternalist, the third a fine old philistine who carved a destiny in ham. But these men gave themselves and their city to business enterprise in its ugliest manifestation. The city of course has its remissions, its loveliness, but the incidental brutality of that enterprise is a main characteristic of the city, a characteristic barely suggested by Mr. Taylor, not clearly imagined by Mr. Hornby in his graceful drawings, so beautifully reproduced.

One would like, as a corrective to Mr. Taylor's pleasant picture, some leaves from Upton Sinclair's Jungle, Jack London's Iron Heel, Frank Norris's Pit, H. K. Webster's Great Adventure, the fiction of Edith Wyatt and Henry Fuller and Robert Herrick and Will Paine and Weber Linn and Sherwood Anderson, the poetry of Edgar Lee Masters and Carl Sandburg, the prose of Jane Addams. No one who looked at the City Council ten years ago, for example, can forget the brutality of that institution of collective life.

They called the old-time aldermen the " gray wolves." They looked like wolves, cold-eyed, grizzled, evil. They preyed on the city South side, West side, North side, making the shaky tenements and black brothels and sprawling immigrant-filled industries pay tribute in twenty ways. One night, curious to see Chicago at its worst, four of us went to a place that was glibly described as " the wickedest place in the world." It was a saloon under the West side elevated, and a room back of the saloon. At first it seemed merely dirty and meager, with its runty negro at the raucous piano. But at last the regular customers collected; the sots, the dead-beats, the human wreckage of both sexes, the woman of a fat pallor, the woman without a nose . . . They surrounded us, piled against us, clawed us. And that, in its way, is Chicago, Stead's Satanic vision of it revealed.

But the other side of that hideousness in Chicago is the thing one loves it for, the large freedom from caste and cant which is so much an essential of democracy, the cordiality which comes with fraternity, the access to men and life of all kinds. Chicago is a scrimmage but also an adventure, a frank and passionate creator struggling with hucksters and hogsters, a blundering friend to genius among the assassins of genius, a frontier against the Europe that meant an established order, an order of succession and a weary bread-line. In Chicago, for all its philistinism, there is the condition of hope that is half the spiritual battle, whatever stockades the puritans try to build. It is that that makes one lament the silence in Mr. Taylor's pleasant book. But the puritanical tradition requires silence. Polite and refined, self-centered and private-minded, attached to property and content within limitations, it made visible Chicago what it is.

THE CLOUDS OF KERRY

IT is the Gulf Stream, they say, that makes
Kerry so wet. All the reservoir of the Atlantic,
at any rate, lies to the west and south, and the prevailing winds come laden with its moisture. Kerry
lifts its mountains to those impinging winds —
mountains that in the sunlight are a living colorful
presence on every side, but cruelly denuded by the
constant rains. For usually the winds flow slowly
from the sea, soft voluminous clouds gathered in
their arms, and as they pass they sweep their drooping veils down over the silent and somewhat melan-
choly land.

In the night-time a light or two may be seen dot-
ted at great intervals on those lonely hillsides, but
for the most part the habitations are in the cooms
or hollows grooved by nature between the parallel
hills. The soil on the mountains is washed away.
The vestiture that remains is a watery sedge, and it
is only by garnering every handful of earth that the
tenants can attain cultivation even in the cooms.
Their fields, often held in common, are so small as
to be laughable, and deep drainage trenches are
dug every few yards. Sometimes in the shifting
sunlight between showers a light-green patch will
loom magically in the distance, witness to man's indefatigable effort to achieve a holding amid the rocks.
An awkward boreen will climb to that holding, and

if one goes there one may find a typical tall spare countryman, bright of eye and sharp of feature, housing in his impoverished cottage a large brood of children. To build with his own hands a water-tight house is the ambition for which this man is slaving, and the slates and cement may be ready there near the pit which he himself has dug for foundation. A yellowish wife will perhaps be nursing the latest baby in the gloomy one-roomed hovel, and as one talks to the man, respectful but sensible, and admirable in more ways than he can ever dream of, one elf after another will come out, bare-legged, sharp-eyed, shy, inquisitive, to peer from far off at the stranger. He may be illiterate, this grave hillside man, but his starvelings go down the boreen to the bare cold schoolhouse, to be taught whatever the pompous well-meaning teacher can put into their minds of an education designed for civil service clerks. The children may be seen down there if one passes at their playtime, kicking a rag football with their bare feet, as poor and as gay as the birds.

There was a time when the iron was deep in these farmers' souls. Eking the marrow from the bones of the land, they were so poor that they had nothing to live on but potatoes and the milk of their own tiny cattle, the Kerry-Dexter breed of cattle that alone can pick a living from that ground. Until twenty-five years ago, I was told, some of the hillside men had never bought a pound of tea in their lives, or known what it was to spend money for clothes. To this day they wear their light-colored homespun, and one will meet at the fairs many fine sturdy middle-aged farmers with a cut to their home-made clothes that reminds one of the Bretons. It

was from these simple and ascetic men, fighting
nature for grim life, that landlords took their rackrents — one of them, the Earl of Kenmare, erecting
a castle at near-by Killarney that thousands of Americans have admired.   The fight against landlordism
was bitter in Kerry.   I met one countryman who was
evicted three times, but finally, despite the remorseless protests of the agent, was allowed to harbor in
a lean-to against the wall of the church.   There
were persecutions and murders, the mailed hand of
the law and the stealthy hand of the assassin.   Even
to-day if that much-evicted tenant had not been sure
of me he would not have spoken his mind.   But
when he was sure, he confided with a winning smile
that at last he had something to live for and work
for, a strip of land that was an " economic holding,"
determined by an Estates Commission which has
shouldered the landlord to one side and estimated
with its own disinterested eyes the large nutritive
possibilities of gorse and heather and rock and bog.

Why do they stay?   But most of them have not
stayed.   Kerry has not one-third the people to-day
that it had seventy years ago.   The storekeeper in
a seaside village where I stopped in Kerry, a little
father of the people if there ever was one, yet had
acted the dubious rôle of emigration agent, and had
passed thousands of his countrymen on to America.
A few go to England.   " For nine years," one hard-
working occupier mentioned to me, " I lived in the
shadow of London Bridge."   But for Kerry, the
next country to America, America is the land of
golden promise.   In a field called Coolnacapogue,
" hollow of the dock leaves," I stopped to ask of a
bright lad the way to Sneem, and he ended by asking

me the way to America. It is west they turn, away from the Empire that " always foul-played us in the past, and I am afeard will foul-play us again."

" The next time you come, please God you'll bring us Home Rule." That is the way they speak to you, if they trust you. They want government where it cannot play so easily the tricks that seared them of old.

I went with a government inspector on one mission in Kerry. At the foot of the forbidding western hills there was a bleak tongue of land cut off by two mountain streams. At times these streams were low enough to ford with ease, but after a heavy rain the water would rise four or five feet in a few hours and the streams would become impassable torrents. For the sake of a widow whose hovel stood on this island the Commission consented to build a little bridge. The concrete piers had been set at either side successfully, but the central pier, five tons in weight, had only just been planted when a rain came, and a torrent, and the unwieldy block of cement had toppled over in the stream. This little catastrophe was the first news conveyed by the paternal storekeeper to the inspector on our arrival in town, and we walked out to see what could be done.

Standing by the stream, we were visible to the expectant woman on the hill. In the soft mournful light of the September afternoon I could see her outlined against the gray sky as she came flying to learn her fate. She came bare of head and bare of foot, a small plaid shawl clasped to her bosom with one hand. Her free hand supported her taut body as she leaned on her own pier and bent her deep

[68]

eyes on us across the stream. As she told in the slow lilting accent of Kerry the pregnant story of the downfall of the center pier, she would cast those eyes to the inanimate bulk of concrete, half submerged in the water, as if to contemn it for lying there in flat helplessness. But she was not excited or obsequious. A woman of forty, her expression bespoke the sternness and gravity of her fight for existence, yet she was a quiet and valiant fighter. She was, I think, the most dignified suppliant I have ever beheld.

If the pier could not be raised, she foresaw the anxieties of the winter. She seemed to look into them through the grayness of the failing light. She foresaw the sudden risings of the stream, the race for her children to the schoolhouse, the risk of carrying them across on her back. And she clung to her children.

"You have had trouble, my poor woman?" the inspector said, knowing that her husband two years before had been drowned in the torrent.

"Aye, indeed, your honor, 'tis I am the pity of the world. One year ago my child was lost to me. It was in the night-time, he was taken with a hemorrhage, with respects to your honor. I woke the children to have them go for to bring the doctor, but it was too late an they returned. He quenched in my arms, at the dead hour of night."

"The pity of the world" she was in truth. The inspector could do nothing until the ground was firm enough to support horses and tackle in the spring. We walked back through the somber bog, the mountains seeming to creep after us, and we speculated on the bad work of the contractor. To

[69]

the storekeeper we took our grievance, and there we came on another aspect of that plaintive acquiescence so strong in the woman. Yes, the storekeeper admitted with instant reasonableness, the inspector was right: Foley had failed about the bridge. "I'll haul him over," he said, full of sympathy for the woman. And he would haul him over. And the pier would lie there all winter.

If the people could feel that this solicitude of the Estates Commission were national, it would bind them to the government. But most of the inspectors are of the landlord world, ruling-class appointees, well-meaning, remote, superior, unable to read between the lines. And so Kerry remains with the old tradition of the government, suspicious of its intentions, crediting what genuine services there are to the race of native officials who alone have the intuition of Kerry's kind.

They want army recruits from Kerry, to defend the Empire; that Empire which meant landlords and land agents and rackrents for so many blind and crushing years. They want those straight and stalwart and manly fellows in the trenches. But Kerry knows what the trenches of Empire are already. It has fought starvation in them, dug deep in the bogs between sparse ridges of potatoes, for all the years it can remember. It is no wonder Kerry cannot grasp at once why it should go forth now to die so readily when it has only just grudgingly been granted a lease to live.

HENRY ADAMS

HENRY ADAMS was born with his name on the waiting list of Olympus, and he lived up to it. He lived up to it part of the time in London, as secretary to his father at the Embassy; part of the time at Harvard, teaching history; most of the time in Washington, in La Fayette Square. Shortly before he was born, the stepping stone to Olympus in the United States was Boston. Sometimes Boston and Olympus were confused. But not so long after 1838 the railroads came, and while Boston did its best to control the country through the railroads there was an inevitable shift in political gravity, and the center of power became Ohio. It was Henry Adams's fate to knock at the door of fame when Ohio was in power; and Ohio did not comprehend Adams's credentials. Those credentials, accordingly, were the subject of some wry scrutiny by their possessor. They were valid, at any rate, at the door of history, and Henry Adams gave a dozen years to Jefferson and Madison. It was his humor afterwards to say he had but three serious readers — Abram Hewitt, Wayne MacVeagh and John Hay. His composure in the face of this coolness was, however, a strange blending of serenities derived equally from the cosmos and from La Fayette Square. He was not

The Education of Henry Adams, an Autobiography. Boston: Houghton Mifflin Co.

above the anodyne of exclusiveness. Even his autobiography, a true title to Olympus, was issued to a bare hundred readers before his death, and was then deemed too incomplete to be made public. It is made public now nominally for " students " but really for the world that didn't know an Adams when it saw one.

For mere stuff the book is incomparable. Henry Adams had the advantage of full years and happy faculty, and his book is the rich harvest of both. He had none of that anecdotal inconsequentiality which is a bad tradition in English recollections. He saved himself from mere recollections by taking the world as an educator and himself as an experiment in education. His two big books were contrasted as *Mont-Saint-Michel and Chartres: A Study of Thirteenth-Century Unity,* and *The Education of Henry Adams: A Study of Twentieth-Century Multiplicity.* The stress on multiplicity was all the more important because he considered himself eighteenth century to start with, and had, in fact, the unity of simple Americanism at the beginning.

Simple Americanism goes to pieces like the pot of basil in this always expanding tale of a development. There are points about the development, about its acceptance of a " supersensual multiverse," which only a Karl Pearson or an Ernst Mach could satisfactorily discuss or criticize. A reader like myself gazes through the glass bottom of Adams's style into unplumbed depths of speculation. Those depths are clear and crisp. They deserve to be investigated. But a " dynamic theory of history " is no proper inhabitant of autobiography, and " the larger synthesis " is not yet so domesticated as the plebeian idea of God. That Adams should conduct his study to these ends is, in one sense, a magnificent culmination. A theory of life is the fit answer to the super-sensual riddle of living. But when the theory must be technical and even professional, an autobiography has no climax in a theory. It is better to revert, as Adams does, to the classic features of human drama: " Even in America, the Indian Summer of life should be a little sunny and a little sad, like the season, and infinite in wealth and depth of tone — but never hustled." It is enough to have the knowledge that along certain lines the prime conceptions were shattered and the new conceptions pushed forward, the tree of Adams rooting itself firmly in the twentieth century, coiled round the dynamos and the law of acceleration.

Whatever the value of his theory, Henry Adams embraced the modernity that gradually dawned on him and gave him his new view of life. Take his fresh enthusiasm for world's fairs as a solitary example. One might expect him to be bored by them, but Hunt and Richardson and Stanford White and Burnham emerge heroically as the dramatizers of America, and Henry Adams soared over their obviousness to a perception of their " acutely interesting " exhibits. He was after — something. If the Virgin Mary could give it to him in Normandy, or St. Louis could give it to him among the Jugo-Slavs and the Ruthenians on the Mississippi, well done. No vulgar prejudices held him back. He who could interpret the fight for free silver without a sniff of impatience, who could study Grant without the least filming of patriotism, was not likely to turn up his nose at unfashionable faiths or to espouse fashion-

able heresies.   He was after education and any century back or forward was grist to his mill.   And
his faith, even, was sure to be a sieve with holes in
it.   " All one's life," as he confesses grimly, " one
had struggled for unity, and unity had always won,"
yet " the multiplicity of unity had steadily increased,
was increasing, and threatened to increase beyond
reason."   Beyond reason, then, it was reasonable to
proceed, and the son of Ambassador Adams moved
from the sanctity of Union with his feet feeling
what way they must, and his eye on the star of
truth.

So steady is that gaze, one almost forgets how
keen it is.   But there is no single dullness, as I remember, in 505 large pages, and there are portraits
like those of Lodge or La Farge or St. Gaudens or
the Adamses, which have the economy and fidelity
of Holbein.   A colorist Adams is not, nor is he
a dramatist.   But he has few equals in the succinct
expressiveness that his historical sense demands, and
he can load a sentence with a world of meaning.
Take, for instance, the phrase in which he denies
unity to London society.   " One wandered about in
it like a maggot in cheese; it was not a hansom cab,
to be got into, or out of, at dinner-time."   He says
of St. Gaudens that " he never laid down the law,
or affected the despot, or became brutalized like
Whistler by the brutalities of his world."   In a
masterly chapter on woman, he summed up, " The
woman's force had counted as inertia of rotation,
and her axis of rotation had been the cradle and
the family.   The idea that she was weak revolted
all history; it was a palæontological falsehood that
even an Eocene female monkey would have laughed

at; but it was surely true that, if force were to be diverted from its axis, it must find a new field, and the family must pay for it. . . . She must, like the man, marry machinery." In Cambridge " the liveliest and most agreeable of men — James Russell Lowell, Francis J. Child, Louis Agassiz, his son Alexander, Gurney, John Fiske, William James and a dozen others, who would have made the joy of London or Paris — tried their best to break out and be like other men in Cambridge and Boston, but society called them professors, and professors they had to be. While all these brilliant men were greedy for companionship, all were famished for want of it. Society was a faculty-meeting without business. The elements were there; but society cannot be made up of elements — people who are expected to be silent unless they have observations to make — and all the elements are bound to remain apart if required to make observations."

Keen as this is, it does not alter one great fact, that Henry Adams himself felt the necessity of making observations. He approached autobiography buttoned to the neck. Like many bottled-up human beings he had a real impulse to release himself, and to release himself in an autobiography if nowhere else; but spontaneous as was the impulse, he could no more unveil the whole of an Adams to the eye of day than he could dance like Nijinski. In so far as the Adamses were institutional he could talk of them openly, and he could talk of John Hay and Clarence Kink and Henry Cabot Lodge and John La Farge and St. Gaudens as any liberated host might reveal himself in the warm hour after dinner. But this is not the Dionysiac tone of autobiography and Henry

Adams was not Dionysiac. He was not limitedly Bostonian. He was sensitive, he was receptive, he was tender, he was more scrod than cod. But the mere mention of Jean Jacques Rousseau in the preface of this autobiography raises doubts as to Henry Adams's evasive principle, " the object of study is the garment, not the figure." The figure, Henry Adams's, had nagging interest for Henry Adams, but something racial required him to veil it. He could not, like a Rousseau or " like a whore, unpack his heart with words."

The subterfuge, in this case, was to lay stress on the word " education." Although he was nearly seventy when he laid the book aside and although education means nothing if it means everything, the whole seventy years were deliberately taken as devotion to a process, that process being visualized much more as the interminable repetition of the educational escalator itself than as the progress of the person who moves forward with it. Moves forward to where? It was the triumph of Henry Adams's detachment that no escalator could move him forward anywhere because he was not bound anywhere in particular. Such a man, of course, could speak of his life as perpetually educational. One reason, of course, was his economic security. There was no wolf to devour him if his education proved incomplete. Faculty *qua* faculty could remain a permanent quandary to him, so long as he were not forced to be vocational, so long as he could speculate on " a world that sensitive and timid natures could regard without a shudder."

The unemployed faculty of Henry Adams, however, is one of the principal fascinations of this altogether fascinating book. What was it that kept Henry Adams on a footstool before John Hay? What was it that sent him from Boston to Mont-Saint-Michel and Chartres? The man was a capable and ambitious man, if ever there was one. He was not merely erudite and reflective and emancipatingly skeptical: he was also a man of the largest inquiry and the most scrupulous inclusiveness, a man of the nicest temper and the sanest style. How could such justesse go begging, even in the United States? Little bitter as the book is, one feels Henry Adams did go begging. Behind his modest screen he sat waiting for a clientage that never came, while through a hole he could see a steady crowd go pouring into the gilded doors across the way. The modest screen was himself. He could not detach it. But the United States did not see beyond the screen. A light behind a large globule of colored water could at any moment distract it. And in England, for that matter, only the Monckton Milneses kept the Delanes from brushing Adams away, like a fly.

The question is, on what terms did Adams want life? It is characteristic of him that he does not specify. But one gathers from his very reticence that he had least use of all for an existence which required moral multiplicity. Where he seems gravest and least self-superintending is in those criticisms of his friends that indicate the sacrifice of integrity. He was no prig. Not one bleat of priggishness is heard in all his intricate censure of the eminent British statesmen who sapped the Union. But there is a fund of significance in his criticism of Senator Lodge's career, pages 418 and on, in which " the larger study was lost in the division of interests and the ambitions of fifth-rate men." It is in a less concerned tone that the New Yorker Roosevelt is discussed. "Power when wielded by abnormal energy is the most serious of facts, and all Roosevelt's friends know that his restless and combative energy was more than abnormal. Roosevelt, more than any other man living within the range of notoriety, showed the singular primitive quality that belongs to ultimate matter — the quality that medieval theology assigned to God — he was pure act." Pure act Henry Adams was not. If Roosevelt exhibited "the effect of unlimited power on limited mind," he himself exhibited the contrary effect of limited power on unlimited mind. Why his power remained so limited was the mystery. Was he a watched kettle that could not boil? Or had he no fire in his belly? Or did the fire fail to meet the kettle? Almost any problem of inhibition would be simpler, but one could scarcely help ascribing something to that refrigeration of enthusiasm which is the Bostonian's revenge on wanton life force. Except for his opaline ethics, never glaring yet never dulled, he is manifestly toned down to suit the most neurasthenic exaction. Or, to put it more crudely, he is emotion Fletcherized to the point of inanition.

Pallid and tepid as the result was, in politics, the autobiography is a refutation of anæmia. There was, indeed, something meager about Henry Adams's soul, as there is something meager about a butterfly. But the lack of sanguine or exuberant feeling, the lack of buoyancy and enthusiasm, is merely a hint that one must classify, not a command that one condemn. For all this book's parsimony, for all its psychological silences and timidities, it is an original contribution, transcending caste and class, combining true mind and matter.   Compare its comment on education to the comment of Joan and Peter — Henry Adams is to H. G. Wells as triangulation to tape-measuring.   That profundity of relations which goes by the name of understanding was part of his very nature.   Unlike H. G. Wells, he was incapable of cant.   He had no demagoguery, no mob-oratory, no rhetoric.   This enclosed him in himself to a dangerous degree, bordered him on priggishness and on egoism.   But he had too much quality to succumb to these diseases of the sedentary soul. He survives, and with greatness.

THE AGE OF INNOCENCE

SWEET and wild, if you like, the first airs of spring, sweeter than anything in later days; but when we make an analogy between spring and youth and believe that the enchantment of one is the enchantment of the other, are we not dreaming a dream?

Youth, like spring, taunts the person who is not a poet. Just because it is formative and fugitive it evokes imagination; it has a bloom too momentary to be self-conscious, vanished almost as soon as it is seen. In boys as well as girls this beauty discloses itself. It is a delicacy as tender as the first green leaf, an innocence like the shimmering dawn, "brightness of azure, clouds of fragrance, a tinkle of falling water and singing birds." People feel this when they accept youth as immaculate and heed its mute expectancies. The mother whose boy is at twenty has every right to feel he is idyllic, to think that youth has the air of spring about it, that spring is the morning of the gods. Youth is so often handsome and straight and fearless; it has its mysterious silences — its beings are beings of clear fire in high spaces, kin with the naked stars. Yet there is in it something not less fiery which is far more human. Youth is also a Columbus with mutineers on board.

As one grows older one is less impatient of the

supposition that innocence actually exists. It exists, even though mothers may not properly interpret it for boys. Its sudden shattering is a barbarism which time may not easily heal. But in reality youth is neither innocence nor experience. It is a duel between innocence and experience, with the attainments of experience guarded from older gaze. Human beings take their contemporaries for granted, no one else: and neither teachers nor superiors nor even parents find it easy to penetrate the veil that innocence and ignorance are supposed to draw around youth.

If youth has borrowed the suppositions about its own innocence, the coming of experience is all the more painful. The process of change is seldom serene, especially if there is eagerness or originality. The impressionable and histrionic youth has incessant disappointment in trying misfit spiritual garments. The undisciplined faculty of make-believe, which is the rudiment of imagination, can go far to torture youthfulness until a few chevrons have been earned and self-acceptance begun.

Do mature people try to help this? Do they remember their own uncertainty and frustration? One of the high points in Mr. Trotter's keen psychological study, Instincts of the Herd in Peace and War, indicates adult jealousy of the young. Mr. Trotter goes beyond Samuel Butler and Edmund Gosse in generalizing their kind of youthful experience. He shows the forces at work behind the patronizing and victimizing of the young.

The tendency to guard children from sexual knowledge and experience seems to be truly universal in civilized man and to surpass all differences of morals, discipline, or taste. . . .

Herd instinct, invariably siding with the majority and the ruling powers, has always added its influence to the side of age and given a very distinctly perceptible bias to history, proverbial wisdom, and folklore against youth and confidence and enterprise and in favor of age and caution, the immemorial wisdom of the past, and even the toothless mumbling of senile decay.

The day will come when our present barbaric attitude toward youth will be altered. Before it can be altered, however, we must completely revise our conventions of innocence. Youth is no more certainly innocent than it is certainly happy, and the conspiracy of silence that surrounds youth is not to be justified on any ground of over-impressionableness. Innocence, besides, can last too long. Every one has pitied stale innocence. If a New York child of ten becomes delirious, his ravings may quite easily be shocking to older people. Already, without any particular viciousness or precocity, he has accumulated a huge number of undesirable impressions, and shoved them under the surface of his mind. What, then, to do? The air of spring that is about him need not mislead his guardians. They may as well accept him as a ripe candidate for a naughty world. Repression, in other words, is only one agent of innocence, and not the most successful. Certainly not the most successful for domesticating youth in the sphere that men and women consider fit to be occupied. If youth is invited to remain innocent long after it recognizes the example and feels the impulses of its elders, the invitation will go unaccepted. Youth cannot read the newspapers or see the moving pictures without realizing a discrepancy between conduct and precept, which is one hint to precept to take off its bib.

This knowingness is not quite what it seems to be. Youth is never so young as when experienced. But those who must deal with it cannot lose by making it more articulate, by saving it from the silly adult exclusions of jealousy and pride. For this jealousy and pride continually operates against youth in the name of dignity and discipline. And so the fiction of happy youth is favored, the fiction that portrays youth as the spring time of the spirit; that pipes a song about a lamb, and leads the lamb to slaughter.

THE IRISH REVOLT

"It may be a good thing to forget and forgive; but it is altogether too easy a trick to forget and be forgiven."— G. K. Chesterton in *The Crimes of England*, 1916.

WHEN a rebellion has failed men say it was wicked or foolish. It is, on the contrary, wickedness and folly to judge in these terms. If men rise against authority the measure of their act cannot be loyalty or prudence. It is the character of the authority against which men revolt that must shape one's mind. No free man sets an ultimate value on his life. No free man sets an ultimate sanction on authority. Is it just authority, representative, tolerable? The only revolt that is wicked or foolish is the revolt against reasonable or tolerable authority. If authority is not livable, revolt is a thousand times justified.

The Irish rebellion was not prudent. Its imprudence did not weigh with the men who took to arms. Had hope inspired them, they would have been utterly insane. But hope did not inspire them. They longed for success; they risked and expected death. The only consequence to us, wrote Padraic Pearse before action, is that some of us may be launched into eternity. "But who are we, that we should hesitate to die for Ireland? Are not the claims of Ireland greater on us than any personal

ones? Is it fear that deters us from such an enterprise? Away with such fears. Cowards die many
times, the brave only die once." To strike a decisive blow was the aspiration of the Irish rebels.
But decisive or not, they made up their minds to
take action before the government succeeded in at-
taching all their arms.

In this rebellion there was no chance of material
victory. Pearse, MacDonagh, Connolly, Clark,
Plunkett, O'Rahilly, O'Hanrahan, Daly, Hobson,
Casement, could only hope against hope. But their
essential objective was not a soldiery. It was an
idea, the idea of unprotested English authority in
Ireland. It was to protest against the Irish nation's
remaining a Crown Colony of the British Empire
that these men raised their republican standard and
under it shed their blood. In the first process of that
revolt few of them were immediately sacrificed.
Their fight was well planned. They made the most
of their brief hour. But when they were captured
the authority they had opposed fulfilled their expecta-
tions to the utmost. Before three army officers,
without a legal defender, each of the leaders was
condemned by court-martial. Their rebellion had
been open. Their guilt was known and granted.
They met, as they expected to meet, death.

The insurrection in Ireland is ended. A cold
tribunal has finished by piecework the task that the
soldiers began. The British Empire is still dominant
in Dublin. But ruthless and remorseless behavior
sharpens the issue between authority and rebellion.
Even men who naturally condemn disorder feel im-
pelled to scrutinize the authority which could deliberately dispense such doom. If that authority de-

served respect in Ireland, if it stood for justice and the maintenance of right, its exaction of the pound of flesh cannot be questioned. It does not represent " frightfulness." It represents stern justice. Its hand should be universally upheld. But if, on the other hand, English authority did not deserve respect in Ireland, if it had forfeited its claims on these Irishmen, then there is something to be made known and said about the way in which this Empire can abuse its power.

Between the Irish people and English authority, as every one knows, there has been an interminable struggle. A tolerable solution of this contest has only recently seemed in sight. The military necessity of England has of itself precluded one solution, the complete independence of Ireland. The desire for self-government in Ireland has opposed another solution, complete acquiescence in the union. Between these two goals the struggle has raged bitterly. But human beings cannot live forever in profitless conflict. After many years the majority of the English people took up and ratified the Irish claims to self-government. In spite of the conservative element in England and the British element in Ireland, the *modus vivendi* of home rule was arranged. It is the fate of this *modus vivendi,* accepted by the majority of Irishmen as a reasonable commutation of their claims, that explains the recent insurrection. These men who are dead were once for the most part Home Rulers. Their rebellion came about as a sequel to the unjust and dishonest handling of home rule.

For thirty-five years home rule has been an issue in Great Britain. The majority of the British peo-

ple supported Gladstone during many home rule
sessions. The lower house of Parliament repeatedly
passed the measure. The House of Lords, however,
turned a face of stone to Ireland. It icily rejected
Ireland's offer to compound her claims. This irreconcilable attitude proved in the end so monstrous
that English Liberalism revolted. It threw its
weight against the rigid body that denied it. It compelled the House of Lords to accept the Parliament
act, its scheme for circumventing the peers' veto.
Then, three times in succession, it passed the home
rule bill.

Every one knows what happened. During the
probation of the bill the forces that could no longer
avoid it constitutionally made up their minds that
they would defeat it unconstitutionally. Men left
the House of Lords and the House of Commons to
raise troops in eastern Ulster. These, not the Irish,
were Germany's primary allies in the British Isles.
Cannon, machine guns, and rifles were shipped to
Ireland. Every possible descendant of the im-
planted settlers of Ireland was rallied. Large numbers were openly recruited and armed. The Ulster
leaders pleaded they were loyal, but they insisted
that the Liberals of England did not and could not
speak for the Empire. The only English authority
they recognized was an authority like-minded to
themselves. Lord Northcliffe joined with Lord
Londonderry and Lord Abercorn and Lord Wil-
loughby de Broke and Lord Roberts and Sir Edward Carson and Bonar Law to advise and stimu-
late rebellion. Some of the best British generals in
the army, to the delight of Germany, were definitely
available as leaders. A provisional government,

with Carson as its premier, was arranged for in 1911. The Unionist and Orange organizations pledged themselves that under no conditions would they acknowledge a home rule government or obey its decrees. In 1912 the Solemn Covenanters pledged themselves "to refuse to recognize its authority." During this period the government negotiated, but took no action. There were no Nationalists under arms.

If free men have a right to rebel, how can any one gainsay Ulster? It was the Ulster contention that home rule would be unreasonable, intolerable, and unjust. This was a prophecy, perhaps a natural and credible prophecy. But it is not necessary to debate the Ulster rebellion. It was a hard heritage of England's crime against Ireland. It is enough to say that English authority refused to abandon the home rule measure and in April, 1914, Mr. Asquith promised to vindicate the law.

The British League for the support of Ulster had sent out "war calls." The Ulster Unionist Council had appropriated $5,000,000 for volunteer widows and orphans. Arms had been landed from America and, it was said, from Germany. Carson had refused to "negotiate" any further. His mobilization in 1914 became ominous. The government started in moving troops to Ulster. The King intervened. Mr. Balfour inveighed against the proposal to use troops. The army consulted with Carson. Generals French and Ewart resigned.

About this period, with Asquith and Birrell failing to put England's pledges to the proof, the National Volunteers at last were being organized. Mr. Asquith temporized further. At his behest John

Redmond peremptorily assumed control of the Volunteers. Their selected leader was Professor MacNeill, a foremost spirit in the non-political Gaelic revival. There was formal harmony until the European war was declared, when Mr. Redmond sought to utilize the National Volunteers for recruiting. This move made definite the purely national dedication of the Irish Volunteers.

Four events occurred in rapid succession to destroy the Irish Volunteers' confidence in English authority. These were decisive events, and yet events over which the Irish Volunteers could have no control.

On July 10th, 1914, armed Ulster Volunteers marched through Belfast, and Sir Edward Carson held the first meeting of his provisional government.

On July 26th, 1914, the British troops killed three persons and wounded thirty-two persons because rowdies had thrown stones at them in Dublin, subsequent to their futile attempt to intercept Irish Volunteer arms.

On Sept. 19th, 1914, the home rule bill was signed, but its operation indefinitely suspended.

In May, 1915, Sir Edward Carson became a member of the British Cabinet.

These events were endured by John Redmond. He had early accepted a Fabian policy and put his trust in Englishmen who shirked paying the price of maintaining the law they decreed. The more radical men in Dublin were not so trusting. They had heard Asquith promise that no permanent division of Ireland would be permitted, and they learned he had bargained for it. They had heard him promise he would vindicate the law, and they saw him sanction the defiant military leader as commander-in-chief and the defiant civil leader as a minister of the crown. With the vivid memory of British troops killing Irish citizens on the streets of Dublin, they drew their conclusions as to English honor. They had no impulse to recruit for the defense on the Continent of an Empire thus honorable. They looked back on the evil history they had been ready to forget. They prepared to strike and to die.

Irishmen like myself who believed in home rule and disbelieved in revolution did not agree with this spirit. We thought southern Ireland might persuade Ulster. We thought English authority was possibly weak and shifty, but benign. We did not wish to see Ireland, in the words of Professor MacNeill, go fornicating with Germany. When our brothers went to the European war we took England's gratitude as heartfelt and her repentance as deep. Our history was one of forcible conquest, torture, rape, enforced subservience, ignorance, poverty, famine. But we listened to G. K. Chesterton about Englishmen in relation to magnanimous Ireland: " It was to doubt whether we were worthy to kiss the hem of her garment."

All the deeper, then, the shock we received from the execution of our men of finest mettle. They were guilty of rebellion in wartime, but so was De Wet in South Africa. There seems to have been a calculation based on the greater military strength of the Dutch. A government which had negotiated with rebels in the North, which had allowed the retention of arms in Ulster, which had put Carson in the Cabinet, could not mark an eternal bias in its judgment of brave men whose legitimate constitutional prospects it had raised high and then intolerably suspended. But this English government, often cringing and supine, was brave enough to slay one imprisoned rebel after another. It did so in the name of " justice," the judges in this rebellion being officers of an army that had refused to stand against rebellion in Ulster.

It is not in vain, however, that these poets and Gaelic scholars and Republicans have stood blindfolded to be shot by English soldiers. Their verdict on English authority was scarcely in fault. They estimated with just contemptuousness the temper of a ruling class whose yoke Ireland has long been compelled to endure. Until that yoke is gone from Ireland, by the fulfillment of England's bond, the memory of this rebellion must flourish. It testifies sadly but heroically that there are still Irishmen who cannot be sold over the counter, Irishmen who set no ultimate sanction on a dishonest authority, Irishmen who set no ultimate value on their merely mortal lives.

A LIMB OF THE LAW

"LOOK here," said the policeman, tapping me on the chest, "Mrs. Trotsky used to live up here above on Simpson Avenue, in three rooms. And then see what happens — she turns up in Stockholm with two million roubles.

"Oh, I don't blame her. But ain't we all human — Socialists, Democrats, Republicans? All we need is a chance.

"I admit, Socialism has beautiful ideas. But are they practical? That's what I ask. Now, pardon me, just a minute! Just one minute, please! Socialism is a fine theory, but look at Emma Goldman. That woman had seven lovers. Free love. Yes, many a time I've heard them, preaching the children belonged to the state. Here's their argument, see, they say that a man and a woman wants to get married but the man figures, have I enough to support her? and the woman figures, how much has he got? and the only thing for them to do in that case is to turn the children over to the state. Now, I ask you, is that human?

"You say, a lot of these women in limousines practice free love without preaching it. Oh, I don't deny it. And, look't here, I'm surprised there isn't more bombs at that. Right here on the Avenue you see the cars in one long procession all day, like every one was a millionaire, and three blocks over you see people who haven't the means of livelihood, without a shirt to their backs. I'm a public offcer, as you might say, and maybe it sounds queer what I'm going to say, but I'm afraid to have my own children on the steps of the apartment house. I takes the night-stick to them and I says, ' Beat it out of here, don't let the landlord see you, or he'll raise the rent again.'

" You said it, something's rotten somewhere. What do you think of the government holding back all that meat, just because the packers want it fixed that way, and plenty of people on the Lower East Side there willing to buy it all up — and at good prices too? But, no, it has to be held back to suit the packers. And then they lower the price a little. Because why? The government lets them have all that meat for what they like.

" It's the same way with the ice. Did you see what they done? The mayor gets them all together, to prevent them boosting the price on it, and it's fixed; they can't raise the price this summer to more than five fifty a ton. They wait two days at the old price, and then they put it at five fifty. Two days they wait, that's all.

" Of course this is the best government in the world. I'll tell you what proves it — all these foreigners coming over here. Look at that soda-fountain man there. You heard him talk up for the Bolsheviki, didn't you? Well, he hasn't much gray matter in here, but just the same that fellow makes as much in three months as I get for a whole lousy year. Three months, and he hasn't been here ten years. And my people been here two hundred. But these immigrants come over ignorant and uneducated, and only down in Kentucky and Tennessee are our people not able to read and write. I hear down there they are regular tribes, fighting each other and all that. Of course that soda-fountain man, he couldn't associate with lots of the people I go with. If he walked in, they'd look at him as much as to say, 'Who have we here?' But he rolls up the coin just the same.

"But the trouble with the Russian people, I'll tell you. Why, eighty per cent of them can't read or write. Now I'll tell you what it's like. It's like this: the Russian people is like a dog was tied up in the back-yard, see, and then he was let loose and he run wild with joy all over the place, and then it depended who was the first to whistle to him, whee-whee, and Lenin and Trotsky they whistled, whee-whee, and the Russian people came right to them. Of course I don't think it'll work. They want to do away with money over there. You know, you want to buy a shoeshine and you give a man a head of cabbage. That's impractical. And then again the government can't own everything. It's all right for public utilities, but you take and try to control everything and what'll happen? It can't be done. What I say is, let a man earn a million or so, and then say to him, anything over and above that million we take away, see? And when he has his million he doesn't go on trying to monopolize everything. But now, you have all these uneducated people around here, and the more money they earn the worse they are.

"I'll tell you. Right across the hall from where my wife and me live there's a lovely woman, a Jewess, one of the nicest people you could want to meet, and I'm in her house and she's in mine all the time, until her husband comes home. But he's one of that kind, you know! The other night he comes home with three friends and he says to me, 'Say, Charlie, come on down to Long Island with us in the car for a week. I'll pay all your expenses!' 'You will, eh,' I says. 'Now I'll tell you something. That sort of thing don't go with me. In the first place, you know I can't get leave to be away from the police department for a week; in the second place, you know I can't leave my wife here; in the third place, you know damn well I can't afford to go with you. I know your kind! You have your three friends here and you want them to see what a great guy you are. Well, I'll tell you what you are,' and I told him. Now he'll be the same if he has a million. And I'll tell you another kind that hasn't respectability. No, I mean decency. She was a big fat woman and her baby was crying here the other day, and she opened her dress right there and leaned down to feed the child. You know, just like that statue, I forget the name. And all the little boys rubbering around. That's the class of people you have to contend with around here in this place, with the air full of fish guts they throw out of the windows, and everything.

" But the German ones are different. Not that I want to praise the Germans or the like of that, but they're self-respectful, you know. It's the lack of education with them others — those others.

" But you put the Socialists in power and what difference will it make? I'm — I'm not against Socialism, I want you to understand. But there's human nature! "

A PERSONAL PANTHEON

NOT long ago, in the Metropolitan Magazine, Clarence Day shied a cocoanut at old Henri Fabre. Personally I had nothing against Henri. I rather liked him. But I was extremely cheered when Clarence said publicly, " that old bird-artist, you don't have to admire him any longer." Without waiting for further encouragement I bounced Henri off the steps of my Pantheon.

Have you a little Pantheon? It is necessary, I admit, but nothing is so important as to keep it from getting crowded with half-gods. For many months my own Pantheon has been seriously congested. Most of the ancient deities are still around — George Meredith and Walt Whitman and Tom Hardy and Sam Butler — and there is a long waiting list suggested by my friends. Joseph Conrad has been sitting in the lobby for several years, hungering for a vacant pedestal, and I have had repeated applications from such varied persons as Tchekov, R. Browning, J. J. Rousseau, Anatole France, Huxley, Dante, Alexander Hamilton, P. Shelley, John Muir, George Washington and Mary Wollstonecraft. But with so many occupants already installed, with so many strap-hangers crushed in, it has been impossible to open the doors to newcomers. My gods are like the office-holders — few die and none resign. And when a happy accident occurs, like the demolition of Henri Fabre, I feel as one feels when some third person is good enough to smash the jardinière.

I was troubled by Woodrow Wilson for a while. Two or three years ago he swept into the Pantheon on a wave of popularity, and there was no excuse for turning him out. He was one of the stiffest gods I had ever encountered. His smile, his long jaw, his smoothness, made him almost a Tussaud figure among the free Lincolns and Trelawnys and William Blakes. I stood him in the corner when he first arrived, debating where to put him, but at no time did I discover a pedestal for him. Young Teddy Junior helped me to like Woodrow. So did Mr. Root and Mr. Smoot. So did Mr. Wadsworth and Mr. Henry Cabot Lodge. But what, after all, had kept Mr. Wilson from being a Republican? How did he differ intrinsically from a Henry Stimson, a Nicholas Murray Butler, a Theodore Burton? The pedestal stood gaping for him, and yet I had not the heart to enthrone him; and never shall I enthrone him now. Now I look upon him with the flat pulse and the unfluttered heart of a common and commonplace humanity. He is President, as was Taft. So is he impressive. But the expectation I had blown up for him is punctured. He would have been a god, despite all my prejudice against his styles, if at any time he had proved himself to be the resolute democrat. But the resolute democrat he was not. He was just an ordinary college president inflating his chest as well as he could, and he has to get out of my Pantheon.

This eviction of the President relieves my feelings like a good spring cleaning. To be con-structive gives me pleasure, but not half so much pleasure as to be de-structive, to cast out the junk of my former mental and spiritual habitations. A great many people are catholic. They have hearts in which Stepping Heavenward abides with Dumas and East Lynne. I envy these people and their receptive natures, but my own chief joy is to asphyxiate my young enthusiasms, to deliver myself from the bondage of loyalty.

There is Upton Sinclair. I was so afraid I was unjust to Upton Sinclair that I almost subscribed to his weekly, and when I saw his new novel, Jimmie Higgins, I actually read it.

" My best book," Mr. Sinclair assures the world. If that is really the case, as I hope, I am happily emancipated from him forever. He is something of an artist. He converts into his own kind of music the muck-rake element in contemporary journalism. He is always a propagandist, and out of religious finance or the war or high society or the stockyards or gynecology he can distill a sort of jazz-epic that nobody can consider dull. But if one is to act on such stimulants, one ought to choose them carefully, and I'd much rather go straight to Billy Sunday than take my fire water from Upton Sinclair. Once on reading his well-known health books, I nearly fasted nine days under his influence. That is to say, I fasted twenty-four hours. The explosions of which I dreamt at the end of that heroic famine convinced me that I was perhaps a coarser organism than Mr. Sinclair suspected, and I resumed an ordinary diet. But until I had a good reason for expelling this uncomfortable idealist from my Pantheon I was always in danger of taking him seriously. Now, I am glad to say, I have a formula for him, and I am safe.

Nietzsche is the kind of sublime genius to whom Upton Sinclair is nothing but a gargoyle; yet the expulsion of Nietzsche was also required. When we used to read the *New Age* ten years ago, with Oscar Levy's steady derision of everything and anything not Nietzschean, I had a horrible sense of inadequacy, and I started out to read the Master's works. It was a noble undertaking, but futile. Slave and worm as I was, I found Nietzsche upsetting all the other fellows in the Pantheon. He and William Blake fought bitterly over the meaning of Christianity. Abraham Lincoln disgusted him with funny stories. He was sulky with George Meredith and frigid with Balzac and absurdly patronizing to Miss Jane Addams. It pained me to get rid of him, but I voted him away.

This Olympian problem does not seem to bother men like William Marion Reedy. Mr. Reedy is the sort of human being who can combine Edgar Lee Masters and Vachel Lindsay, single tax and spiritualism, Woodrow Wilson and Theodore Roosevelt. He knows brewers and minor poets and automobile salesmen and building contractors and traffic cops and publishers, and he is genuinely himself with all of them. He finds the common denominator in machine politicians and hyperacid reformers, and without turning a hair he moves from tropical to arctic conversation. He is at home with Celtic fairies and the atomic theory, with frenzied finance and St. Francis. If he has a Pantheon, and I believe he has, it must be a good deal like a Union depot, with gods coming in and departing on every train

[99]

and he himself holding a glorious reception at the information booth. I am sure he can still see the silver lining to W. J. Bryan and the presidential timber in Leonard Wood. He does not make fun of Chautauqua. He can drink Bevo. He has a good word for Freud. He has nothing against Victorianism. And yet he is a man. This receptivity puzzles me. A person with such open sympathies is called upon to slave in their service, to rush here and there like a general practitioner, to sleep with a watch under his pillow and a telephone at his head. How does he find the energy to do it! I admire it. I marvel at men who understand all and forgive all, who are as omnivorous as Theodore Roosevelt, as generous and many-sided as Walt Whitman. Think of those who have a good word to say for Bonar Law! It is less democratic, I am sure, to run a hand-picked Pantheon, but it saves a lot of much-needed vitality. Give me a temple on a high hill, with a long drop down from the exit.

NIGHT LODGING

IT is sadly inept, not to say jejune, to accuse Maxim Gorki's Night Lodging of "gloom." Gloomy plays there certainly are. Twin Beds was one of the gloomiest plays I ever saw, and what about a play like She Walked in Her Sleep? That defunct comedy was as depressing as a six-day bicycle race. Night Lodging is somber. No one denies that. But to believe that a somber play must necessarily be a " gloomy " play is like believing that Christmas must necessarily be unpleasant. It simply isn't true, and to suppose it is mentally inelastic.

But the trouble is, we are mentally inelastic. We say, Ah yes, Strindberg, the woman-hater; or Ibsen, the man who bites on granite; or Gorki, the Big Gloom; when as a matter of fact these artists are simply human beings who have got beyond the comprehensions of the fifth grade. This is itself an old story in criticism. Only the story has to be re-told every time the New York newspaper critics are called upon to characterize a serious drama. With a regularity as unfailing as the moon, the New York critics reaffirm their conviction that a play concerning derelict human beings must of course be squalid, sodden, high-brow and depressing. It is mentally ruinous to believe and assert such things, yet their belief and assertion are endemic in the New York newspapers, like malaria in the jungle or goiter in the Alps.

Mr. Arthur Hopkins's presentation of Night Lodging at the Plymouth Theatre may or may not be better than the presentation some time ago at the German theatre. I do not know. I never saw the performance at the German theatre and I am inclined to distrust the persons to whom the German theatre is not so much a thing in itself as a stick with which to whack the American theatre. But, better or worse than the German performance, Mr. Hopkins's is to the good. It is a strong, firm, spacious, capable performance, resting not so much on a few pinnacles as on a general level of excellence. It is presented bravely. Making no attempt to sweeten the drama to the taste of American critics, it allows the resolute sincerity of Gorki to penetrate every word and action of the performance. The result is undoubtedly not Russian, even if every actor in the cast talks with a semblance of foreignness. But the result is viable, Russian or not. A sense of human incident and human presence is quickly secured, and after that there comes a stream of events which never loses its reality either in force or direction. The impact is tremendous. Gorki inundates one's consciousness with these human fortunes and misfortunes of his tenement basement. And while occasional accents slip awry in the tumult of his creation, the substance of his story finds one a corroborator — in a way that one simply never corroborates depression or gloom.

The men and women, who come together in this night lodging of a Russian city, are of the emancipated kind that one sees on the benches in Madison Square. They are recruited from the casual worker and the non-worker, the unemployed and the unem-

ployable, the loafers and the criminals and the broken
and the déclassé. On the first evening when one
hears their voices through the murk of the ill-lit basement, one realizes that their anarchism is bitter.
They grate on one another, sneer at one another,
bawl at one another, tell one another to go to hell.
They are earthly pilgrims whose burdens have galled
them. They do not understand or accept their fate.
They are full of self-pity. They are, in a word,
one's tired and naked self. But this relaxed and
wanton selfness is projected by a Russian who keeps
for his people the freshness of childhood — a freshness charming in some cases, horrible in others, but
always with a touch of immortality. How they reveal themselves in this nudity of common poverty!
A woman in the corner is coughing, coughing. She
wants air. Her husband does not go to her. His
patience is snapped. In the middle of the room lies
a man half recovered from a drunken brawl. He
aches loudly with stale liquor and stale wounds. In
the other corner a youth dreams of his mistress, the
wife of the lodging-house keeper — a mistress from
whom he pines to escape. The "baron" sits in the
shadow, telling of his high antecedents, to weary
sarcastic listeners. Elsewhere the broken young actor repeats the medical verdict that his organism is
poisoned with alchohol. "You mean 'organon,'"
shouts another. "No, organism. My organism . . ." And so, these lives sweep round and
round in an eddy of helpless egotism, the sport of
the winds of heaven.

Then arrives a leonine old man, a philosophical
patriarchal wanderer. Quite simply he fits into this
life of the basement, but unlike the rest he is no

longer self-centered or self-afflicted. He walks erect in his anarchism. And gradually the lives of the night lodging group around him. He sits by the dying woman. He talks of women to the young thief, and talks of the fine life in rich Siberia that is beckoning to the young. He stands like an untroubled oak in the gales that toss the others hither and thither. Lord, he has seen life! And he meets them all with compassion, a man among children.

He goes. His presence has not prevented the lodging-house keeper's wife from driving the young man to kill her husband. Nor has it prevented that flashing devil from mutilating her sister whom the young man really loves. But though the old man departs he leaves after him a rent of blue in the clouds that choke these people's lives. One after another the night lodgers question life afresh under the wanderer's influence. The tartar's arm is still smashed. The kopecks are still scarce. Nastia is still helpless. The baron is still reminiscent. The actor is still alcoholic. But there is aroused in the night lodging the imperishable dream of happiness, and no one is ready to quench it.

Why is the grave and beautiful play *not* gloomy? It is not enough to say that the really gloomy play gives a naturalistic version of life which the spectator rejects as false. Nor is it enough to say that the falsity of a sodden play consists not in its shadows or in its discords but in its absence of the vitamen of beauty. Many plays are denied truth because their truth is not agreeable. Many plays are denied beauty simply because their beauty is a stranger. Yet we know that truth or beauty may be as sable as the night, as icy as the pole, as lonely as a waterfall in the wilderness. The fact is, gloom is the child of ingrained ugliness, not the child of accidental, conventional ugliness. It is the people who think too narrowly of poverty and failure who see Night Lodging as depressing. It does not fail in beholding life. It is not poor in sympathy.

YOUTH AND THE SKEPTIC

In 1912, I think it was, Mr. Roosevelt told the public how Mr. Taft had bitten the hand that fed him. I have forgotten Mr. Taft's rejoinder but it was a hot rejoinder and it led to some further observations from the colonel. Those were the days. Nothing but peace on earth and good will among Republicans.

About that time I happened to have lunch with a most attractive young man, one of the first American aviators. He was such a clear-cut young man, with trusting brown eyes and no guile in him. And said he to me, " But how can these things be true? I can't understand it. If any one else said these things you'd pay no attention to them, but both of these men are fine men; they've both been president; and if these things they say *are* true, then neither of them can be such fine gentlemen. I can't make it out, honestly." And he looked at me with a profundity of pained inquiry.

What could I say? What can you say when you meet with such simple faith? It took years of primary school and Fourth of July and American history to build up this conception of the American presidents, and now the worst efforts of a president and an ex-president had only barely shaken the top-structure. What was the good of forcing this youth to unlearn everything he had learned? If I took away his faith in the divine office of president, perhaps he might begin to lose his patriotism and his willingness to lay down his life for the flag. Perhaps he might go on and lose faith in the jury system, the institution of marriage, the right of free speech, the sacred rights of property, the importance of Harvard. Faith is a precious but delicate endowment. If I unhinged this lad's faith, perhaps he would follow in the footsteps of Martin Luther, Voltaire, Anatole France, Bernard Shaw and Emma Goldman — the " Goldman Woman " as the Ochs man and the Pulitzer man and the Ogden Mills Reed man call her in their outbursts of American chivalry. I wanted no such arid and lonely career for this splendid young man. I hated to think of his wearing an ironic smile like Anatole France or losing his fresh bloom to be a subversive idealist like Eugene Debs. Much better, said I to myself, that he should hug Taft to his bosom, even if mistaken, than that he should repulse him and face life without him. So I gave the lad soothing words and earnest though insincere glances, and he went his way puzzled but greatly reassured.

Now, I ask you, did I do wrong? You may say that simple faith is all very well, but a man ought to live in the real world and know his way around. Otherwise he is incapable of handling the existing situation. He is compelled to evade uncomfortable facts. Very true. Quite right. Exactly so. But is it better to be able to face facts at the cost of being a nerveless skeptic, or to be something of a simpleton and yet a wholesome man of action, a man of will and character and pep? What is the good of knowing facts, especially unflattering and unpalatable facts, if it confuses you and upsets you and undermines everything you've been brought up to believe? What's the use? Voltaire may be all right in his way, but is his way the only way? Can we all be Voltaires?

If I stick up for good faith in the character of presidents, I know that there will be a bad comeback. I know the tricks of the skeptic. But even if my opponents use their ugliest arguments, am I therefore to give in to them? I refuse to admit that there is nothing else than to destroy a beautiful faith in the good that is everywhere.

What the skeptics do, of course, is to use the old argument of the war. They say: Yes, your fine brown-eyed trustful young aviator is a typical product of patriotism. And where were the prime examples of patriotism to be found? In Germany. He happens, in your instance, to believe in the divine office of the presidents. But it is much more characteristic of him to be on his knees to the Kaiser. Yet consider how one-sided you are. When he declares himself ready to die for the Kaiser you see the joke. You see the joke when he is pouring out his reverence over the Tsar of Russia or the Tsar of Bulgaria or the King of Greece. But when it comes to an American you say, "Oh, don't let's destroy this beautiful faith! How precious it is, how noble, how commendable! Hands off, please." And you act in the same way toward the Constitution or the Supreme Court. It's magnificent when the Germans come ahead with a perfectly good new constitution, model 1920. But we must stick to the brand of 1789, with the cow-catcher added in 1910. Hail to Our Iron Constitution! And hail to the Old Man's

Home down in Washington where they hand out the uncontaminated economics that they themselves lisped at the Knees of the Fathers of Our Country. Straight from the source, these old men got their inspiration, and they are a credit to the early nineteenth century. You think we exaggerate your loyalty? You agree that the simple faith of young Germans and young Turks can be highly dangerous, but do you counsel unquestioned faith for young Americans?

That is the argument, rather ingenious in its way; but hardly likely to fool the intelligent, law-abiding, God-fearing citizen. Because no good American could admit for one instant that the cases are on all fours. America, after all, is a democracy. And when a young man starts out having faith in a democracy he is in an altogether different position from Germans and Turks and Bulgarians and Soviet Russians and people like that. A democracy, whatever its faults, is founded in the interests of all the people. It is unquestionable. Therefore simple faith in it is equivalent to simple faith in a first principle; and you cannot go behind first principles.

That, in the end, is the trouble with the skeptic. He thinks it is very clever to question the things that are of the light in just the same spirit that he questions things that are of the darkness. And of course he goes wrong. He is like a surgeon who cuts away the sound flesh rather than the diseased flesh. He is, in the evergreen phrase, de-structive not con-structive.

And so I am glad that I did not seek to disillusion my fine young aviator. If I had succeeded in disillusioning him, who can tell what the consequences might have been? We know that during the war there were grim duties to be performed by our young men — towns to be bombed where it took excessive skill to kill the men-citizens without killing the women and the children. If I had sapped this boy's faith even one pulsation, perhaps he would have failed in his duty.

You cannot be too careful how you lead people to rationalize. In this world there is rationalism and plenty of it. But is there not also a super-rationalism? And must we not always inculcate super-rationalism when we *know* we possess the true faith?

THE SPACES OF UNCERTAINTY

OR, AN ACHE IN THE VOID

[Inscribed to the *Little Review*]

THE floor, unfortunately, was phosphorus, so he had to pick his steps with care. But at last he came to a French window, which he opened, and sprang to a passing star. Star, not car. He was a poet, and that is what young poets do.

He had a pleasant physiognomy, as young men go. Unformed, of course — perhaps twenty minutes late and the hall only two-thirds full. But he was no longer young enough to hang his hat on the gas. He was from the East via Honey Dew, Idaho, but he had long resided with an aunt in Nebraska and so was a strong Acutist. He wore gray shirts and a lemon tie. At Harvard — he went to Harvard — he had opened his bean with considerable difficulty and crushed in a ripe strawberry of temperament. So that he could never stop himself when he beheld a passing star.

The motion was full, with significant curves. It made him a little air-sick at first, but he preferred air-sickness. He made no compromise with the public taste for pedestrianism. After a few days that quickly ceased to be solar, he was rewarded. He came to Asphodelia, a suburb of Venus on the main line.

In Asphodelia the poets travel on all-fours, kick their heels toward Mercury, and utter startling cries. In Asphodelia a banker lives in the menagerie, and they feed mathematical instructors through a hole in the wall. This new participant had too much of the stern blood of the Puritan in his rust-proof veins to kick more than one heel at a time, but when he observed a gamboling Asphodelian of seventy years he felt a little wishful, and permitted himself a trifling ululation. The local cheer-leader heard him and knew him at once for a Harvard Acutist, and there was joy in Asphodelia.

A year or so sufficed him. He grew tired of sleeping in the branches of the cocoanut tree, and the river of green ink wearied him. So when the next star swung around he slipped away from his pink duenna and crept into the lattice-work to steal his passage home.

Thought slid from him like an oscillant leaf. He hung there lonely, in his Reis underwear, aching in the void.

He alighted in the harbor of Rio. When he trans-shipped to New York in ordinary ways, he prepared his Yonkers uncle, and he was met in undue course on Front Street.

"My boy," said his uncle, "what do you want me to do for you? Speak the word. You have been gone so long, and you were given up for lost."

"Only one thing do I want," confessed the former Acutist.

"And what might that be?" the uncle more circumspectly inquired.

"Take me at once to the great simple embrace of wholesome Coney Island."

So, clad in an Arrow collar and a Brokaw suit, the young poet stepped from Acutism on to the Iron Boat.

And what is the moral of this tale, mes enfants? . . . But must we not leave something to waft in the spaces of uncertainty?

WILLIAM BUTLER YEATS

I AM sorry now not to have treasured every word that came from my poet. At the moment I disliked to play Boswell; I thought it beneath my dignity. But artists like Arnold Bennett who ply the note-book are not ashamed to be the Boswells of mediocrity. Why should I have hesitated to take notes of William Butler Yeats?

In the Pennsylvania station I had met him, as his host agreed, and I intruded on him as far as Philadelphia. I say intruded: his forehead wrinkled in tolerant endurance too often for me to feel that I was welcome. And yet, once we were settled, he was not unwilling to speak. His dark eyes, oblique and set far into his head, gave him a cryptic and remote suggestion. His pursed lips closed as on a secret. He opened them for utterance almost as in a dream. As if he were spokesman of some sacred book spread in front of him but raptly remembered, he pronounced his opinions seriously, occasionally raising his hands to fend his words. He was, I think, inwardly satisfied that I was attentive. I was indeed attentive. I had never listened to more distinguished conversation. Or, rather, monologue — for when I talked he suspended his animation, like a singer waiting for the accompanist to run down.

It was on the eve of The New Republic. I asked him if he'd write for it, and he answered characteristically. He said that journalism was action and that nothing except the last stage of exasperation could make him want to write for a journal as he had written about Blanco Posnet or The Playboy. The word " journalism " he uttered as a nun might utter " vaudeville." He was reminded, he said, of an offer that was made to Oscar Wilde of the editorship of a fashion paper, to include court gossip. Wouldn't it interest Wilde? " Ah, yes," responded Wilde, " I am deeply interested in a court scandal at present." The journalist (devourer of carrion, of course) was immediately eager. " Yes," said Wilde, " the scandal of the Persian court in the year 400 B. C."

It was telling. It made me ashamed for my profession. I could not forget, however, pillars of the *Ladies' World* edited by Oscar Wilde which I used to store in an out-house. Wilde had condescended in the end.

Yeats's mind was bemused by his recollection of his fellow-Irishman. Once he completed his lectures he would go home, and a " fury of preoccupation " would keep him from being caught in those activities that lead to occasional writing. His lectures would not go into essays but into dialogues, " of a man wandering through the antique city of Fez." In the cavern blackness of those eyes I could feel that there was a mysterious gaze fixed on the passing crowd of the moment, the gaze of a stranger to fashion who might as well write of Persia, a dreamer beyond space and time.

" And humanitarian writing," he concluded, with a weary limp motion of his hand, " the writing of reformers, ' uplifters,' with a narrow view of de-

[115]

mocracy I find dull. The Webbs are dull. And truistic."

I spoke of the Irish John Mitchel's narrow anti-democracy and belief in the non-existence of progress, such as he had argued in Virginia during the Civil War. Mitchel, he protested, was a passionate nature. The progress he denied was a progress wrongly conceived by Macaulay and the early Victorians. It was founded on "truisms" not really true. Whether Carlyle or Mitchel was the first to repudiate these ideas he didn't know: possibly Mitchel was.

Yeats's one political interest at that time, before the war, was the Irish question. He believed in home rule. He believed the British democracy was then definitely making the question its own, and "this is fortunate." I spoke of Jung's belief in England's national complex. He was greatly interested. Ulster opposition to home rule he regretted. "The Scarlet Woman is of course a great inspiration," he said, "and Carson has stimulated this. His one desire is to wreck home rule, and so there cannot be arrangement by consent. I agree with Redmond that Carson has gone ahead on a military conspiracy. Personally, I do not say so for a party reason. I am neither radical nor tory. I think Asquith is a better man than Lloyd George — less inflated. He is a moderate, not puffed up with big phrases. He meets the issue that arises when it arises. . . . I object to the uplifter who makes other people's sins his business, and forgets his chief business, his own sins. Jane Addams? Ah, that is different."

His lectures he would not discuss but he spoke a

good deal of audiences. In his own audiences he found no one more eager, no one who knows more, than an occasional old man, a man of sixty. He was surprised and somewhat disappointed to find prosperity go hand in hand with culture in this country. In the city where the hotel is bad there is likely to be a poor audience. Where it is good, the audience is good. In his own country the happiest woman he could name was a woman living in a Dublin slum whose mind is full of beautiful imaginings and fantasies. Is poverty an evil? We should desire a condition of life which would satisfy the need for food and shelter, and, for the rest, be rich in imagination. The merchant builds himself a palace only for auto-suggestion. The poor woman is as rich as the merchant. I said yes, but that a brute or a Bismarck comes in and overrides the imagination. He agreed. " Life is the warring of forces and these forces seem to be irreconcilable."

It could cost an artist too much to escape poverty. I spoke of the deadness of so much of the work done by William Sharp and Grant Allen. He said it was Allen's own fault. He, or his wife, wanted too many thousand dollars a year. They had to bring up their children on the same scale as their friends' children! And he kindled at this folly. " A woman who marries an artist," he said with much animation, " is either a goose, or mad, or a hero. If she's a goose, she drives him to earn money. If she's mad she drives him mad. If she's a hero, they suffer together, and they come out all right."

Phrases like this were not alone. There was the keen observation that the Pennsylvania station is " free from the vulgarity of advertisement "; the admission of second hand expression in Irish poetry except in The Dark Rosaleen and Hussey's Ode; a generalization on Chicago to the effect that " courts love poetry, plutocracies love tangible art." Not for a moment did this mind cease to move over the face of realities and read their legend and interpret its meaning. Meeting him was not like Hazlitt's meeting Coleridge. I could not say, " my heart, shut up in the prison-house of this rude clay, has never found, nor will it ever find, a heart to speak to; but that my understanding also did not remain dumb and brutish, or at length found a language to express itself, I owe to Coleridge." But the Yeats I met did not meet me. I remained on the periphery. Yet from what I learned there I can believe in the sesame of poets. I hope that some one to-day, nearer to him than a journalist, is wise enough to treasure his words.

"WITH MALICE TOWARD NONE"

LAST night I woke up suddenly to the sound of bombardment. A great detonation tore the silence; an answering explosion shook it; then came a series of shots in diminishing intensity. My windows look out on a rank of New York skyscrapers, with a slip of sky to the south. In the ache of something not unlike fear, I thrust out my head to learn as quickly as I could what was happening. No result from the explosions was to be seen. The skyscrapers were gaunt and black, with a square of lost light in a room or two. The sky was clean-swept and luminous, the stars unperturbed. Still the shots barked and muttered, insanely active, beyond the blank buildings, under the serene sky.

I heard hoarse cries from river-craft. Could it be on the river? Could it be gun practice, or was there really an interchange of gun-fire? A U-boat? An insurrection? At any rate, it had to be explained and my mind was singularly lively for three a. m.

Long after your country has gone to war, I told myself, there remains, if you have sluggish sympathies, what may fairly be called a neutrality of the imagination. You are aware that there is fighting, bloodshed, death, but you retain the air of the philosophic. You do not put yourself in the place of Americans under fire. But if this be really bombardment, shell-fire in Manhattan? I felt in an instant how Colonel Roosevelt might come to seem the supreme understander of the situation. An enemy that could reach so far and hit so hard would run a girdle of feeling from New York to the remotest fighters in Africa or Mesopotamia. To protect ourselves against the hysteria of hatred — that would always be a necessity. But I grimly remembered the phrase, "proud punctilio." I remembered the President's tender-minded words, "conduct our operations as belligerents without passion," and his pledge of sincere friendship to the German people: warfare without "the desire to bring any injury or disadvantage upon them." Here, with the Germans' shell-fire plowing into our buildings and into our skins? Here, meeting the animosity of their guns?

Becoming awake enough to think about the war, I began to reason about this "bombardment," to move from the hypnoidal state, the Hudson Maxim-Cleveland Moffett zone. The detonations were continuing, but not at all sensationally, and soon they began to shape themselves familiarly, to sound remarkably like the round noises of trains shunting, from the New York Central, carried on clear dry November air. Soon, indeed, it became impossible to conceive that these loud reverberations from the Vanderbilt establishment had ever been so distorted by a nightmare mind as to seem gun-fire. And my breathless inspection of the innocent sky!

But that touch of panic, in the interest of our whole present patriotic cultural attitude, was not to be lost. It is the touch, confessed or unconfessed, that makes us kin. If we are to retain toward

German art and literature and science an attitude
of appreciation and reciprocation, without disloyalty,
it must be in the presence of the idea of shell-
wounds German-inflicted. Any other broad-mindedness is the illusory broad-mindedness of the smooth
and smug. It is Pharisaical. It comes from that
neutrality of the imagination which is another name
for selfish detachment, the temperature of the snake.

A generation less prepared than our own for the
mood of warfare it would be difficult to imagine —
less prepared, that is to say, by the situation of our
country or the color of our thought. To declare
now that New York has made no provision for the
air-traffic of the future is not to arouse any sense
of delinquency. No greater sense of delinquency
was aroused ten or fifteen years ago by the bass
warnings of military men. It is not too much to say
that Lord Roberts and Homer Lea were felt to have
an ugly monomania. In that period Nicholas
Murray Butler and Elihu Root and Andrew Carnegie
were thinking in terms of peace palaces. Colonel
Roosevelt had tiny ideas of preparedness, but he was
far more busy enunciating the recall of judges —
and he earned the Nobel Prize. Few men, even two
years ago, believed we would be sending great armies
to Europe in 1917. In the first place, men like
Homer Lea had said that the United States could
not mobilize half a million soldiers for active service in less than three years. And in the next place,
we still felt pacifically. We had lived domestic life
too long ever to imagine our sky black and our grass
red.

Because of this mental unpreparedness for war,
this calm enjoyment of an unearned increment of

peace, there was never a greater dislocation of standards than our recent dislocation, and never a greater problem of readjustment. For England, at any rate, there was a closeness to the war that helped to bring about an alignment of sentiment. But here, besides the discrepancies in the entailment of services, there are enormous discrepancies in sentiment to start with, and policies still to be accepted and cemented, and European prejudices to be suppressed or reconciled. Misunderstanding, under these circumstances, is so much to be looked for, especially with impetuous patriots demanding a new password of allegiance every minute, that the wonder is not at how many outrages there are, but how few.

Most of these outrages fall outside the scope of literary discussion, naturally. " Let the sailor content himself with talking of the winds; the herd of his oxen; the soldier of his wounds; the shepherd of his flocks "; the critic of his books. But there is one kind of outrage that requires to be discussed, from the point of view of culture, if only because there is no ultimate value in any culture that has to be subordinated to the state. That is the outrage, provisionally so-called, of mutilating everything German; not only sequestering what may be dangerous or unfriendly and vindictive, but depriving of toleration everything that has German origin or bears a German name. The quick transformation of Bismarcks into North Atlantics, of Kaiserhofs into Café New Yorks, is too laughable to be taken seriously. The shudderings at Germantown, Pa., and Berlin, O., and Bismarck, N. D., are in the same childlike class. But it is different when an Austrian artist is not permitted to perform because, while we are not at war with Austria, she is our enemy's ally. It is different when " the music of all German composers will be swept from the programmes of scheduled concerts of the Philadelphia Orchestra in Pittsburgh. 'The Philadelphia Orchestra Association wishes to announce that it will conform with pleasure to the request of the Pittsburgh Association. The Philadelphia Orchestra Association is heartily in accord with any movement directed by patriotic motives.'" It is this sort of thing, extending intolerance to culture, that suggests we have been surprised in this whole matter of culture with our lamps untrimmed.

In a sense we, the laissez faire generation, have been unavoidably surprised — so much so that our "proud punctilio" has been jogged considerably loose. So loose, in fact, that we have given up any pretension to being so punctilious as soldiers used to be. It used to be possible, even for men whose hands dripped with enemy blood, to sign magnanimous truces; but science has made another kind of warfare possible, and the civilian population of the modern State, totally involved in a catastrophe beyond all reckoning, falls from its complacency into a depth of panic and everywhere believes that the enemy is inhuman in this war.

Were such beliefs special to this war, hatred might well go beyond the fervor of the Inquisition, and the hope of exterminating the Germans as a people might be universally entertained. But no one who has read history to any purpose will trust too far to this particular emotionality of the hour. To say this, in the middle of a righteous war, may sound unpatriotic. But, if hatred is the test, what could

[123]

be more traitorous and seditious than Lincoln's Second Inaugural Address: "Both read the same Bible, and pray to the same God; and each invokes his aid against the other. . . . The prayers of both could not be answered — that of neither has been answered fully. The Almighty has his own purposes. 'Woe unto the world because of offenses! for it must needs be that offenses come; but woe to that man by whom the offense cometh.' If we shall suppose that American slavery is one of those offenses which, in the Providence of God, must needs come, but which, having continued through his appointed time, he now wills to remove, and that *he gives to both North and South this terrible war, as the woe due to those by whom the offense came,* shall we discern therein any departure from those divine attributes which the believers in a living God always ascribe to him? Fondly do we hope — fervently do we pray — that this mighty scourge of war may speedily pass away. Yet, . . . so still it must be said, 'The judgments of the Lord are true and righteous altogether.' With malice toward none; with charity for all; with firmness in the right, as God gives us to see the right, let us strive on to finish the work we are in; to bind up the nation's wounds; to care for him who shall have borne the battle, and for his widow, and his orphan — to do all which may achieve and cherish a just and lasting peace among ourselves, and with all nations." It is, perhaps, like quoting the Lord's Prayer. And yet it is the neglected wisdom of a man who had gleaned it from long meditating fratricidal war.

But, you may say, Prussia has always been outside humanity. We are engaged in a war foreordained and necessary, a natural war. A war inescapable, yes, but not inevitable. Let the plain testimony of hundreds of books speak. . . . To ask for such discriminations as this is, however, scarcely possible. It is too much, in the face of superstitions, anxieties, and apprehensions, to expect the attitude of culture to be preserved. In peace-time we are allowed to go outside our own state to enjoy any manifestation of the seven arts; and such violent nationalism as attacked The Playboy of the Western World in New York is at once called " rowdy " and " despicable." But in time of war it is part of its morality, or immorality, that culture must be subordinate to clamor, and that even national sculpture must become jingoistic, making railsplitters neatly respectable and idealizing long feet. How far this supervision of culture goes depends only on the degree of pressure. It may go so far as to make the domination of political considerations, state considerations, paramount in everything — precisely the victory that democracy, hoping with Emerson that " we shall one day learn to supersede politics by education," has most to fear.

It is in war itself, with its enmity to so much that is free, that one must seek the opposition to enemy culture, not in the culture that is opposed. Must one, on this account, think any peace a good peace? To do so is to show an immunity from the actual which is not to be envied. It is only necessary to imagine New York bombarded, as many French and English and Belgian and Russian towns have been bombarded since the beginning of the war, to realize the rush of resistance that is born in mankind, expedient for government to recruit and to rally to the end. But for the man who has partaken of democratic culture this " end " involves democracy. All character and all spirit cannot be absorbed in the will to cure the homicidal enemy by his own poison. The only course open to the man who is still concerned for democratic culture is to remember the nobility of Lincoln's example — by concentrating on the offenses rather than the persons that cause the mighty scourge of war, to avoid the war-panic and war-hatred which will enrage our wounds.

WAR EXPERTS

" War is not now a matter of the stout heart and the strong arm. Not that these attributes do not have their place and value in modern warfare; but they are no longer the chief or decisive factors in the case. The exploits that count in this warfare are technological exploits; exploits of technological science, industrial appliances, and technological training. As has been remarked before, it is no longer a gentleman's war, and the gentleman, as such, is no better than a marplot in the game as it is played."— Thorstein Veblen in *The Nature of Peace.*

ACROSS a park in Washington I followed the leisurely stride of two British officers. Their movement, punctuated by long walking-sticks, had a military deliberation which became their veteran gray hairs. They were in khaki uniforms and leather leggings, a red strip at the shoulder marking them as staff officers. Amid groups of loitering nurses and tethered infants and old men feeding pop-corn to the birds they were as of a grander race of men. After a pang of civilian inferiority I asked who they were and learned that one of them was simply a Canadian lawyer — and that, being a judge advocate, he was obliged to boot and spur himself in his hotel bedroom every morning and ride up and down the elevator in polished leggings, for the good of the cause. Never in his life had he heard a machine-gun fired. Never had he flourished anything more dangerous than his family carving knife. On inspection his companion looked similarly martial. The only certain veteran in the parklet was a shrunken old pensioner feeding tame robins on the grass.

Part of the politico-military art is window-dressing of this description. It excites the romantic populace, composed of pedestrians like myself, and serves to advertise the colors. It suggests a leonine order of values from which the shambling citizen is debarred. But back of the window-dressing, the rhetoric of costume and medal and prepared ovation and patriotic tears, there is a reality as different from these appearances as roots are different from flowers. If I had ever supposed that the gist of war was to be derived solely from contemplating uniformed warriors, I came to a new conclusion when I overheard the cool experts of war.

These experts, such of them as I happened to overhear, had come with the British mission to America, and they were far other than the common notion of lords of war. The most impressive of them was a slight figure who reminded me externally of the Greek professor in Bernard Shaw's Major Barbara. Before the war he had been a don at Cambridge, a teacher of economics, and he retained the lucid laboratory manner of an expert who counts on holding attention. It was not in him, as it is in so many older pooh-bah professors, to expect a deference to personal garrulity; but one gained an impression that no words were likely to be wasted on vacuous listeners by a person with such steel-gray eyes.

From London, since the beginning of the war, this

concentrated man had gone out of Paris, to Rome, to Petrograd, to join counsel with various allies on the science of providing munitions. It would never have occurred to any pork packer to employ this fine-faced, sensitive, quiet-voiced professor to work out the economic killing of cattle. Yet almost as soon as he had volunteered in England he began on the task of adapting industry to slaughter, and there was no doubt whatever that his inclusive mind had procured the quick and effective killing of thousands of human beings. It was a joy, strange to say, to listen to him. He was one of those men whom H. G. Wells used to delight in imagining, the sort of man who could keep cool in a cosmic upheaval, his mind as nimble as quicksilver while he devised the soundest plan for launching the forces of his sphere. There was no more trace of priesthood in him than in a mechanic or a chauffeur. He deliberated the organizing of America for destructiveness as an engineer might deliberate lining a leaky tunnel with copper, and there was as little pretension in his manner as there was sentiment or doubt. His accent was cultivated, he was obviously a university man, but he had come to the top by virtue of mental equipment. "Mental equipment" means many things, but plainly he was not of those remote academicians who go in for cerebral scroll-saw work. He managed his mind as a woodman manages an ax. The curt swing and drive and bite of it could escape no one, and for all his almost plaintively modest demeanor he had instant arresting power. It was he and a few men like him who had made it feasible for amateur armies to loop round an empire a burning rain of steel.

[129]

This master of munitions was not the only school-man who had demonstrated brains. There was another professor, this time the purchaser of guns. He had come to his rôle from holding the kind of position that Matthew Arnold once had held. A meager figure enough, superficially the scholastic-dyspeptic, he had shown that the bureaucracy of education was no bad beginning for ordering a new department with small attention to the tricks of merchandise, but with every thought as to technological detail. The conversation that went about did not seem to engage this man, except as it turned on such engrossing topics as the necessity for circumventing child labor. For the rest he was as a soft silent cloud that gathered the ascending vapors, and discharged itself in lightning decision which made no change in the obscurity from which it came.

Under a lamp at night on Connecticut Avenue I saw one late-working member of the mission stop wearily to fend off American inquisition. A training in the Foreign Office had given this distinguished exile a permanent nostalgia for Olympus — and how Olympian the British Foreign Office is, few Americans dare to behold. The candidature to this interesting service of a great democracy is limited to a "narrow circle of society" by various excellent devices, the first of which is that official conditions of entry fix the amount of the private means required at a minimum of £400 a year. "The primary qualification for the diplomatic service," says one friendly interpreter of it, "is a capacity to deal on terms of equality with considerable persons and their words and works. Sometimes, very rarely, this capacity is given, in its highest form, by something which is hardly examinable — by very great intellectual powers. Ordinarily, however, this capacity is a result of nurture in an atmosphere of independence. Unfortunately, it is scarcely too much to say that the present constitution of society provides this atmosphere of independence only where there is financial independence. In a very few cases freedom of mind and character is achieved elsewhere, but then a great price, not measurable by money, has to be paid for it — how great a price only those who have paid it know. . . . The 'property qualification' is operative as a means of selecting a certain kind of character; no readjustment of pay could be a substitute for it. Undoubtedly, as thus operative, it imposes a limitation, but the limitation imposed is not that of a class-prejudice or of a mere preference for wealth — it is a limitation imposed by the needs of the diplomatic service, and those needs are national needs." Out of such a remarkable background, so redolent of " the present constitution of society," my exiled diplomat took his weary stand before prying writers for the press. They wanted to know " the critical shrinking point." They wished to discuss the " maximum theoretic availability." He had no answer to make; he merely made diplomatic moan. In the heavy dispatch box that he set at his feet there were undoubtedly treasured figures, priceless information for Germany in her jiu jitsu of the sea. That dispatch box might have been solid metal for any effect it had on the conversation. He was a kind of expert who took interrogation with pallid mournfulness; who punctuated silence with, " Look here, you've got hold of absolutely the wrong man. . . . Hanged if

I know. . . . My dear sir, I haven't the very faintest idea."

And yet this member of a caste was only coming through because he too was paying a technological price. Wheat and nitrate and ore and rubber — there was nothing his country might need which did not occupy him, staff officer of vital trafficking, throughout numbered nights.

There were a few business men on the mission — mighty few considering their lordship in times of peace. Most of the dominant figures either from Oxford or Cambridge, there was one other intellectual who stood out as rather an exception to the prevailing type. He was an older man whose nature brimmed with ideas, a Titan born to laughter and high discourse and a happy gigantic effervescence. If a reputation brayed too loudly at him, he named its author an ass. If liberalism were intoned to him, he called it detestable and cried to knock the English *Nation's* head against the *Manchester Guardian's*. Yet he was distinguished from most of his colleagues as a radical who afforded wild opinions of his own. To the organization of his country he had contributed one invaluable idea, and each problem that came up in turn he conducted out of its narrow immediate importance into the perspective of a natural philosophy. Not fond of a prearranged system, he irked more than the run of his countrymen at the stuffiness of badly bundled facts. With a great sweep of vigor he would start at the proposition of handling war industry, for example, on a basis not inadequate to the requirements; and out of his running oration would come a wealth of such suggestions as spring only from a cross-fertilizing habit of mind.

These are a handful of England's experts in war-time. They do not bear the brunt of the fight, like the soldiers, but the roots of the flower of war are in just such depths as employ these hidden minds.

OKURA SEES NEWPORT

OKURA was sent to me by Jack Owen, a friend of mine in Japan. Jack said that Okura was taking two years off to study democracy, and would I steer him around. I was delighted. I offered Okura his choice of the great democratic scene, with myself as obedient personal conductor. He was very nice about it in his perfect silver-and-gray manner, and he asked if we could begin with Newport. I suspected a joke, but his eye never twinkled, and so to Newport we went.

The dirty little Newport railway station interested Okura. So did the choked throat of Thames Street, with its mad crush of motors and delivery wagons and foot passengers, and the riotous journey from the meat market to the book shop and from the chemist's to the Boston Store. I explained to Okura that this was not really Newport, only a small sample of the ordinary shopping country town, with the real exquisiteness of Newport tucked away behind. Okura clucked an acceptance of this remark, and our car wove its difficult way through the narrow lane till we returned to Bellevue Avenue.

The name Bellevue Avenue had to be expounded to Okura. He expected a belle vue, not a good plain plutocratic American street. When I told him what to expect, however, he was intensely occupied with its exhibition of assorted architecture, and he broke into open comment. "So very charming!" he cried politely. "So like postcards of Milwaukee by the lake!" I enjoyed his naïve enthusiasm and let it go.

He wanted to know who lived on the avenue, and I told him all the names I could think of. He had heard many of them, the samurai of America being known to him as a matter of course, and he picked up new crumbs of information with obvious gratitude.

"Vanderbilt? Oh, yes." That was old. So were Astor and Belmont.

After a while Okura wrinkled his brow. "I do not see the McAlpin mansion."

"The McAlpins? I have never heard of them," I murmured indulgently.

"But that is one name I think I remember correctly," Okura answered with visible anxiety. "The Bellevue-Astors, the Bellevue-Belmonts, the Bellevue-Stratfords? Please forgive me, I do not understand. Are not the McAlpins also Bellevue-McAlpins?"

It was hard to convince Okura that this was not a Valhalla of hotel proprietors, but at last he got it straight. We went back again as far as the Casino, and I took him in to see the tennis tournament.

Unknown to Okura, I was forced to take seats up rather far — well, to be frank, among the Jamestown and Saunderstown people. But happily we had Newport in the boxes right below us. Some of the ladies sat facing the tennis, some sat with their backs to it, and a great buzz of conversation reverberated under the roof of the stand and billowed on to the court. On the court two young men strove against each other with a skill hardly to be matched in any other game, and occasionally, when something eccentric or sensational happened, a ripple passed through the crowd. But the applause was irregular. People had to be watched and pointed out. It was important to note which human oyster bore the largest pearl. The method of entry and exit was significant, and significant the whole ritual of being politely superior to the game.

Okura was fascinated by the game, unfortunately, and there was so much conversation he was rather distracted.

"I hope it does not annoy you?" I asked him.

"Oh, not at all, thank you very much. It is so democratic!"

At this point the umpire got off his perch, and came forward to entreat the fine ladies.

"I have asked you before to keep quiet," he wailed. "For God's sake, will you stop talking?"

"How very interesting," murmured Okura.

"Yes," I said, "the religious motif."

"Ah, yes!" he nodded, very gravely.

Later on his compatriot Kumagae was to play, and we decided to return to the tournament; but first we took ourselves to Bailey's Beach.

Bailey's Beach is a small section of the Atlantic littoral famous for its seaweed. The seaweed is of a lovely dark red color. It is swept in in large quantities, together with stray pieces of melon-rind and other picnic remnants, and it forms a thick, juicy carpet through which one wades out to the more fluid sea. By this attractive marge sit the ladies in their wide hats and dresses of filmy lace, watching the more adventurous sex pick his way out of the vegetable matter. In the pavilion of the bath-houses sit still less adventurous groups.

It took some time to explain to Okura why this beach, once devoted to the collection of seaweed for manure, should now be dedicated to bathing. But he grasped the main point, that it was a private beach.

" Forgive me," he said, " I see no Jews."

" That's all right," I answered. " You are study-ing democracy. There are no Jews here. None allowed."

" Oh! " he digested the fact. Then his eye brightened. " Ah, you have your geisha girls at the swim-beach. How very charming! "

" No," I corrected him. " Those are not our geisha girls. That is the ' shimmy set.' You know: people who are opposed to the daylight saving act and the prohibition amendment."

" Oh, I understand. Republicans," he nodded happily.

As the Servants' Hour was approaching at Bailey's Beach, and as I had no good explanation to give of it to Okura, I thought we might walk along by the ocean before lunch. Okura was entranced by the walk, and by the fact that it ran in front of these private houses, free to the public as to the wind. Once or twice we went down below stone walls, with everything above hidden from us, but this was exceptional. Okura thought the walk a fine example of essential democracy.

" And what are those long tubes? " he asked, as we gazed out toward Portugal.

" Sewer pipes," I said bluntly, looking at the great

series of excretory organs that these handsome democratic mansions pushed into the sea.

"Are they considered beautiful?" asked Okura.

"Quite," I told him. "They are one of the
features provided strictly for the public."

"So kind!" said the acquiescent Japanese.

We went to lunch with a friend of mine whose
plutocracy was not entirely intact, and but for one
instructive incident it was an ordinary civilized meal.
That incident, however, shall live long in my memory because of my inability to interpret it to Okura.

We had just finished melon, the six of us who sat
down, when the third man was called to the telephone.

He came back, napkin in hand, and said to his
hostess, "I'm awfully sorry, I've got to leave."

His hostess looked apprehensive. "I hope it's
nothing serious?"

"Oh, not at all; please don't worry," he responded, plumping down his napkin, "but I've just
had a message from Mrs. Jinks. She's a man short
and she wants me to come over to luncheon. So
long. Awfully sorry!"

"What did that mean, please?" Okura inquired,
as we hurried back to see Kumagae play.

"Do you mean, democratically?"

"Yes."

"I give it up," I retorted.

"But Mr. Owen said you would want to interpret everything democratic to me," Okura ventured
on, "and is there not some secret here hidden from
me? I fear I am very stupid."

Democratically, I repeated dully, I could not explain.

"But," pressed Okura, "'the world has been made safe for democracy.' I want so much to understand it. I fear I do not yet understand Newport."

And he looked at me with his innocent eyes.

THE CRITIC AND THE CRITICIZED

IT is the boast of more than one proud author, popular or unpopular, that he never reads any criticism of his own work. He knows from his wife or his sorrowing friends that such criticism exists. Sometimes in hurrying through the newspaper he catches sight of his unforgettable name. Inadvertently he may read on, learning the drift of the comment before he stops himself. But his rule is rigid. He never reads what the critics say about him.

Before an author comes to this admirable self-denial he has usually had some experience of the ill-nature and caprice of critics. Probably he started out in the friendliest spirit. He said to himself, Of course I don't profess to *like* criticism. Nobody likes to be criticized. But I hope I am big enough to stand any criticism that is fair and just. No man can grow who is not willing to be criticized, but so long as criticism is helpful, that's all a man has a right to ask. Is it meant to be helpful? If so, shoot.

After some experience of helpful criticism, it will often occur to the sensitive author that he is not being completely understood. A man's ego should certainly not stand in the way of criticism, but hasn't a man a right to his own style and his own personality? What is the use of criticism that is based on the critic's dislike of the author's personality? The critic who has a grudge against an author simply because he thinks and feels in a certain way is scarcely likely to be helpful. The author and the critic are not on common ground. And the case is not improved by the very evident intrusion of the critic's prejudices and limitations. It is perfectly obvious that a man with a bias will see in a book just what he wants to see. If he is a reactionary, he will bolster up his own case. If he is a Bolshevik he will unfailingly bolshevize. So what is the use of reading criticism? The critic merely holds the mirror up to his own nature, when he is not content to reproduce the publisher's prepared review.

The author goes on wondering, " What does he say about me? " But the disappointments are too many. Once in a blue moon the critic " understands " the author. He manages, that is to say, to do absolutely the right thing by the author's ego. He strokes it hard and strokes it the right way. After that he points out one or two of the things that are handicapping the author's creative force, and he shows how easily such handicaps can be removed. This is the helpful, appreciative, perceptive critic. But for one of his kind there are twenty bristling young egoists who want figs to grow on thistles and cabbages to turn into roses, and who blame the epic for not giving them a lyric thrill. These critics, the smart-alecks, have no real interest in the author. They are only interested in themselves. And so, having tackled them in a glow of expectation that has always died into sulky gloom, the author quits reading criticism and satisfies his natural curiosity about himself by calling up the publisher and inquiring after sales.

For my own part, I deprecate this behavior without being able to point to much better models. Critics are of course superior to most authors, yet I do not know many critics who like to be criticized. It does not matter whether they are thin-skinned literary critics or the hippopotami of sociology. They don't like it, much. Some meet criticism with a sweet resourcefulness. They choke down various emotions and become, oh, so gently receptive. Others stiffen perceptibly, sometimes into a cautious diplomacy and sometimes into a pontifical dignity that makes criticism nothing less than a personal affront. And then there is the way of the combative man who interprets the least criticism as a challenge to a fight. The rare man even in so-called intellectual circles is the man who takes criticism on its merits and thinks it natural that he should not only criticize but be criticized.

The pontifical man is not necessarily secure in his ego. His frigid reception of criticism corresponds to something like a secret terror of it. His air of dignity is really an air of offended dignity: he hates being called on to defend himself in anything like a rough-and-tumble fight. He resents having his slow, careful processes hustled and harried in the duel of dispute.

To hand down judgments, often severe judgments, is part of the pontifical character. But the business of meeting severe judgments is not so palatable. As most men grow older and more padded in their armchair-criticism, they feel that they become entitled to immunity. The Elder

Statesmen are notorious. The more dogmatic they are, the more they try to browbeat their critics. They see criticism as the critic's fundamental inability to appreciate their position.

If you are going to be criticized, how take it? The best preparation for it is to establish good relations with your own ego first. If you interpose your ego between your work and the critic you cannot help being insulted and injured. The mere fact that you are being subjected to criticism is almost an injury in itself. You must get to the point where you realize the impregnability of your own admirable character. Then the bumblings of the critic cannot do less than amuse you, and may possibly be of use. He is not so sweet a partisan as yourself, yet he started out rather indifferent to you, and the mere fact that he is willing to criticize you is a proof that he has overcome the initial inhumanity of the human race. This alone should help, but more than that, you have the advantage of knowing he is an amateur on that topic where you are most expert — namely, yourself. Be kind to him. Perhaps if you are sufficiently kind he may learn that the beginning of the entente between you is that he should always start out by appeasing your ego.

BLIND

HE was, in a manner of speaking, useless. He could tend the furnace and help around the house — scour the bath-tub and clean windows — but for a powerful man these were trivial chores. The trouble with him, as I soon discovered, was complete and simple. He was blind.

I was sorry for him. It was bad enough to be blind, but it was terrible to be blind and at the mercy of his sister-in-law, Mrs. Angier. Mrs. Angier ran the rooming-house. She was a grenadier of a woman, very tall and very bony, with a virile voice and no touch of femininity except false curls. She wore rusty black, with long skirts, and a tasseled shawl. Her smile was as forced as her curls. She hated her rooming-house and every one in it. Her one desire, insane but relentless, was to save enough money out of her establishment to escape from it. To that end she plugged the gaps in the bathroom, doled out the towels, scrimped on the furnace, scrooged on the attendance. And her chief sacrifice on the altar of her economy was Samuel Earp, her brother-in-law. Since he was blind and useless, he was dependent on her. When she called, he literally ran to her, crying, " Coming, coming! " He might be out on the window-sill, risking his poor neck to polish the windows that he would never see, but, " Do I hear my sister calling me? Might I —

would you be so good — ah, you are very kind. Coming, Adelaide, just one moment . . ." and he would paddle down stairs. She treated him like dirt. Sometimes one would arrive during an interview between them. The spare, gimlet-eyed Mrs. Angier would somehow manage to compel Samuel to cringe in every limb. He was a burly man with a thick beard, iron-gray, and his sightless eyes were hidden behind solemn and imposing steel-rimmed spectacles. Usually, with head lifted and with his voice booming heartily, he was a cheerful, honest figure. I liked Samuel Earp, though he was a most platitudinous Englishman. But when Mrs. Angier tongue-lashed him, for some stupidity like spilling a water-bucket or leaving a duster on the stairs or forgetting to empty a waste-basket, he became infantile, tearful, and limp. Her lecturing always changed to a sugared greeting as one was recognized. " Good e-e-evening, isn't it a pleasant e-e-evening? " But the only value in speaking to Mrs. Angier was that it permitted Samuel somehow to shamble away to the limbo of the basement.

Of course I wanted to know how he became blind. Luckily, as Mrs. Angier had prosperous relatives in another part of Chicago, she sometimes could be counted on to be absent, and on those occasions or when she went to church, Samuel haunted my room. He was unhappy unless he was at work, and he managed to keep tinkering at something, but I really believe he liked to chatter to me: and he was more than anxious to tell me how his tragedy had befallen him.

" Oh, dear, yes," he said to me, " it happened during the strike. They hit me on the head, and left me unconscious. And I have never seen since, not one thing."

"Who hit you, Samuel?"

"Who hit me? The blackguards who were out on strike, sir. They nearly killed me with a piece of lead pipe. Oh, dear, yes."

It seemed an unspeakable outrage to me, but in Samuel there was nothing but a kind of healthy indignation. He was not bitter. He never raised his voice above its easy reminiscent pitch.

"But what did you do to them? Why did the strikers attack you? What strike was it?"

"I did nothing at all to them. But, you see, my horse slipped and when I was helpless on the ground with my hip smashed, one of them knocked me out. It was right up on the sidewalk. I had gone after them up on the sidewalk, and I suppose the flags were so slippery that the horse came down."

"But what were you doing on a horse?" I asked in despair.

"I was a volunteer policeman. These scoundrels were led by Debs, and we were out to see that there was law and order in Chicago."

"Oh, the Pullman strike. Were you railroading then?"

"Railroading? No, sir, I was in the wholesale dry-goods business. We had just started in in a small way. I was married only two years, to Adelaide's younger sister. Ah, my accident brought on more trouble than she could stand. She was very different from Adelaide, quite dainty and lively, if you follow me. We were living at that time on Cottage Grove Avenue, on the south side. I was building up the importing end of the business, and then this thing came, and everything went to smash. They gave me no compensation whatsoever, to make the thing worse."

" But, Samuel, how did you come to be out against the strikers?"

" And why shouldn't I be out, I'd like to know!" Samuel straightened up from rubbing a chair, and pointed his rag at my voice. " These scoundrels had nothing against Mr. Pullman. He treated them like a prince. But they took the bit in their teeth, and once they break loose where are we? The President didn't get shut of them till he sent in the troops. But I've always contended that if we business men had taken the matter in hand ourselves and nipped the trouble in the bud, we'd have had no such lawlessness to deal with in the end. It is always the same. The business men are the backbone of the community, but they don't recognize their responsibility! Take the sword to those bullies and blackguards; that's what I say!"

The old man lifted both fists like a dauntless Samson, and fixed me with his sightless eyes. He had paid hellishly for living up to his convictions, and here they seemed absolutely unshaken.

" That's all right, too, Samuel," I said, feebly enough, " but how do you feel now? Nobody compensated you for being laid out in that big strike, and your business was ruined, and here you are emptying the waste-basket. How about that? I think it's fierce that you got injured, but those men in the Pullman strike weren't out to break up society. They were fighting for their rights, that's all. Don't you think so now?"

" *No,* sir. The solid class of the community must

be depended upon to preserve law and order. I think that it was the duty of the business men of Chicago to put down ruffianism in that strike and to smite whenever it raised its head. Smite it hip and thigh, as the saying is. Oh, no. Young men have fine notions about these things, ha, ha! You'll excuse me, won't you, but you can't allow violence and disorder to run riot and then talk of men's ' rights ' as an excuse. Ah, but it was a great misfortune for me, I confess. It was the end of all my hopes. The doctors thought at first that the sight might be restored, but I have never seen a glimmer of light since. But we mustn't repine, must we? That'd never do."

"Samuel!" Mrs. Angier's sharp voice pierced the room.

"Good gracious, back so soon. You'll excuse me, I'm sure . . . Coming, Adelaide, coming!"

He groped for his bucket, with its seedy sponge all but submerged in the dirty water. The water splashed a little as he hurriedly made for the door.

"Oh, dear," he muttered, "Adelaide won't like that!"

"AND THE EARTH WAS DRY"

LIKE all great ideas it seemed perfectly simple when Harrod first disclosed it to his unimportant partner John Prentiss.

" Of course we'll get back of it. We've got to," said Harrod, in the sanctity of the directors' room. " You've been down to Hopeville on pay day. It's the limit. Ordinary days there's practically no trouble. Pay day's a madhouse. How many men, do you think, had to have the company doctor last pay day? '

" You don't expect me to answer, Robert," Prentiss replied mildly. " You're telling me, you're not arguing with me."

" Twenty-five, Prentiss, twenty-five drunken swine. What do you think happened? I'll tell you. That doctor never stopped a minute taking stitches, sewing on scalps, mending skulls. He was kept on the hop all day and night all over the town. I'll tell you something more." The sturdy Harrod rapped his fist on the mahogany table, leaning out of his armchair. " The doctor's wife told me a Polack came to her shack at two in the morning with half his thumb hanging off, bitten off in a drunken brawl. What do you think she did, Prentiss? She amputated it herself, on her own hook, just like a little soldier. She's got nerve, let me tell you. But do you think we want to stand

[149]

for any more of this? Not much. Hopeville is going dry!"

Mr. Harrod produced a gold pen-knife and nicked a cigar emphatically. He brushed the tiny wedge of tobacco from his plump trouser leg on to the bronze carpet. He lit his cigar and got up to have a little strut.

Poor Prentiss looked at him as only a weedy Yankee can look at a man whose cheeks are rosy with arrogant health. Why the stout Harrod who ate and drank as he willed should be proclaiming prohibition, while the man with a Balkan digestive apparatus should be a reluctant listener, no one could have analyzed. It never would have occurred to Prentiss to be so restlessly efficient. But Harrod was as simple as chanticleer. He'd made up his mind.

"We'll back Billy Sunday. His advance agent will be in town this week," Mr. Harrod unfolded. "We'll put the whole industry behind him. Drink is a constant source of inefficiency. It's an undeniable cause. When do we have accidents? On Mondays, regularly. The men come back stupefied from the rotgut they've been drinking, and it's simple luck if they don't set fire to the mine. The Hopeville mine is perfectly safe. Except for that one big disaster we had, it's one of the safest mines in the country. But how can you call any mine safe if the fellows handling dynamite and the men working the cage are just as likely as not to have a hangover? We'll stop it. We'll make that town so dry that you can't find a beer bottle in it. It took me some time to realize the common sense of this situation, but it's as clear as daylight; it's ridiculously clear. We're fools, Prentiss, that we didn't advocate prohibition twenty years ago."

"Twenty years ago, Robert," Prentiss murmured, "you were checking coal at the pit-head. You weren't so damned worried about evolving policies for the mine owners twenty years ago."

"Well, you know what I mean," Robert Harrod rejoined.

"Perfectly," retorted Prentiss. "And I'm with you, though all the perfumes of Arabia won't cleanse these little hands."

That was the first gospel, so to speak, and Harrod was as good as his word. He saw Sunday's advance agent, he rallied the industry, he lunched with innumerable Christians and had a few painful but necessary political conferences. The prohibitionist manager he discovered to be a splendid fellow — direct, cleancut, intelligent indefatigable. The whole great state was won to prohibition after a strenuous preparation and a typically "bitter" campaign.

And everything went well at Hopeville. At first, not unnaturally, there was a good deal of rebellion. A few of the miners — you know Irish miners, born trouble-makers — talked considerably. Something in them took kindly to the relief from monotony that came with a periodic explosion, and they muttered blasphemously about the prohibitionists, and time hung heavy on their hands. A few of them pulled out, preceded by the gaunt Scotchman who had run the bare "hotel" where most of the whisky was consumed. These were led by a sullen compatriot of their own, a man who once was a fine miner but who had proved his own best customer in the liquor business and whose contour suggested that his body was trying desperately to blow a bulb. One miner left for a neighboring state (still wet) to purchase a pair of boots. He crawled back on foot after a week, minus the new boots, plus a pawn-ticket, and most horribly chewed by an unintelligent watchdog who had misunderstood his desire to bor-row a night's lodging in the barn. The drinking haunts were desolate reminders of bygone enter-tainments for weeks after the law took effect, and few of the younger men could look forward to tame amusement, amusement that had no elysium in it, without a twinge of disgust. But on the whole, Hopeville went dry with surprising simplicity. A great many of the miners were neither English, Scotch, Cornish, Welsh nor Irish, but Austrians and Italians and Poles, and these were not so inured to drinking and biting each other as Mr. Harrod might have thought. The mud in Hopeville, it is true, was often from nine inches to four feet deep, and there were no named streets, and no known amusements, and a very slim possibility of distrac-tion for the unmarried men. After prohibition, however, a far from unpleasant club house was founded, with lots of " dangerous " reading ma-terial, and a segregated place for home-made music, and bright lights and a fire, and a place to write letters, and a pungent odor of something like syndi-calism in the air.

That was the beginning. The men did not de-tonate on pay day, except in lively conversation. There was less diffused blasphemy. It concentrated rather particularly on one or two eminent men. And when the virtues and defects of these men were

sufficiently canvassed, the " system " beyond them
was analyzed. Even the delight of the Hunkies in
dirt, or the meanness of certain bosses, began to
be less engrossing than the exact place in the ter-
restrial economy where Harrod and Prentiss got
off.

"Well, Robert," inquired the man of migraine,
back in the home office, " how is your precious
prohibition working? It seems to me the doctor's
wife is the sole beneficiary so far."

"Working?" the rubicund Harrod responded
urgently. " I don't know what we're going to do
about it. You can't rely on the men for anything.
A few years ago, after all, they took their wages
over to Mason and blew it all in, or they soaked up
enough rum in Hopeville to satisfy themselves, and
come back on the job. Now, what do they do?
They quit for two weeks when they want to. They
quit for a month at a time. And still they have a
balance. You can't deal with such men. They're
infernally independent. They're impudent with
prosperity. I never saw anything like it. We can't
stand it. I don't know what we're going to do."

"You're going to back the liquor trade, Robert,
of course. That's simple enough."

"You may laugh, but it is too late, I tell you,
the harm's done. We can't remedy it. National
prohibition is right on top of us. I don't know what
we'll do."

"Sell 'em Bevo. That'll keep them conservative.
Ever drink it?"

"Bevo? Conservative? Prentiss, this is serious. These men are completely out of hand."

"Well, aren't they more efficient?"

[153]

"Of course they're more efficient. They're too damnably efficient. They wanted Hopeville drained and they're getting it drained. They'll insist on having it paved next. They'll want hot and cold water. They'll want bathtubs. That'll be the end."

"The end? Come, Robert, perhaps only the beginning of the end."

"It's very amusing to you, Prentiss, but you're in on this with me. We've forced these working-men into prohibition, and now they're sober, they're everlastingly sober. They're making demands and getting away with it. We've got to go on or go under. Wake up, man. I've played my cards. What can we do?"

"What can we do? That is not the point now. Now the point is, what'll *they* do."

TELEGRAMS

IN my simple world a cablegram is so rare that I should treasure the mere envelope. I should not be likely to resurrect it. It would be buried in a bureau, like a political badge or a cigar-cutter — but there is a silly magpie in every man, and a cable I would preserve. To discuss cablegrams or even cut-rate wireless, however, would be an affectation. These are the orchids of communication. It is the ordinary telegram I sing.

There was a magnificence about a quick communication in the days before the Western Union. Horsemen went galloping roughshod through scattering villages. It was quite in order for a panting messenger to rush in, make his special delivery, and drop dead. This has ceased to be his custom. In Mr. Veblen's Theory of the Leisure Class there is one omission. He neglected to deal with that great adept in leisure, the messenger-boy. "Messenger-boy" is a misnomer. He is either a puling infant or a tough, exceedingly truculent little ogre of uncertain age and habit. His life is consecrated. He cares for nothing except to disprove the axiom that a straight line is the shortest distance between two points. Foreseeing this cult of the messenger service, the designers of the modern American city abandoned all considerations of beauty, mystery, and suggestion in an heroic effort to circumvent the boy in blue. But the boy in blue cannot be beaten. By what art he is selected I know not. Whether he is attributable to environment or heredity I dare not guess. But with a possible inferiority to his rival, the coat-room boy, and, of course, nature's paradox the crab, he is supreme.

It is not a telegram in its last stages that has magic. Much better for the purposes of drama to have Cleopatra receive a breathless minion, not a laconic imp with a receipt to be signed. Yet a telegram has magic. If you are hardened you do not register. It is the fresh who have the thrill. But no one is totally superior to telegrams. Be you ever so inured, there is one telegram, *the* telegram, which will find your core.

Sometimes at a hotel-desk I stand aside while an important person, usually a man but occasionally a woman, gets a handful of mail without any sign of curiosity, and goes to the elevator without even sorting out the wires. Such persons are marked. They are in public life. It is pardonable. There must be public men and public women. I should not ask any one to give up his career for the peculiar ecstasies of the telegram. But no one can deny that these persons have parted with an essence of their being. What if I find a solitary notice? " It is under your door." I bolt for the elevator, thrilled, alive.

It may be suggested that my over-laden predecessors are not in public life; that they are very distinguished, very wealthy personages, receiving private advices as to their stocks, their spouses, their children, their wine-bin, their plumbing, or any other of their responsibilities, accessories, possessions. With every deference I answer that you are mistaken. Unless their riches are in a stocking, these are the custodians of tangible goods and chattels. Their title may be secure, but not their peace of mind. Whatever they wish, they are obliged to administrate. Whoever their attorney, the law of gravitation keeps pulling, pulling at their chandeliers. And so in some degree they are connected with, open to, shared by, innumerable people. Without necessarily being popular, they are in the center of populace. They have to meet, if only to repel, demands. I do not blame them for thus being public characters. It is often against their desires. But being called upon to convert a part of their souls into a reception-room, a place where people can be decently bowed out as well as in, it follows that they give up some of their ecstatic privacy in order to retain the rest. This I do not decry. For certain good and valuable considerations one might be induced to barter some of one's own choice stock of privacy, but for myself I should insist on retaining enough to keep up my interest in telegrams. To be so beset by Things as to be dogged by urgent brokers and punctilious butlers, no.

"There's a telegram upstairs for you, sir." "A telegram? How long has it been here?" "It came about half an hour ago." "Ah, thank you. . . . No, never mind, I'm going upstairs." What may not this sort of banality precede? Perhaps another banality, in ink. But not always. A telegram is an arrow that is aimed to fly straight and drive deep. Whether from friend or rival, whether verdict or appeal, it may lodge where the heart is, and stay. From an iron-nerved ticker the message has come, singing enigmatically across the country. But there is a path that leaps out of the dingy office to countless court-rooms, business buildings, homes, hospitals. That office is truly a ganglion from which piercing nerve-fibers curve into the last crevices of human lives. When you enter it to send a telegram it may depress you. You submit your confidence across a public counter. But what does it matter to a creature glazed by routine? He enumerates your words backwards, contemptuous of their meaning. To him a word is not a bullet — just an inert little lump of lead.

Some messages come with a force not realizable. Tragedy dawns slowly. The mind envisages, not apprehending. And then, for all the customary world outside, one is penned in one's trouble alone. One remembers those sailors who were imprisoned in a vessel on fire in the Hudson. Cut off from escape, redhot iron plates between them and the assuaging waters on every side, they could see the free, could cry out to them, could almost touch hands. But they had met their fate. It is strange that by a slip of paper one may meet one's own. There are countries to-day where the very word *telegram* must threaten like a poisoned spear. And such wounds as are inflicted in curt official words time is itself often powerless to heal. As some see it, dread in suspense is worse than dreadful certainty. But there are shocks which are irreparable. It is cruel to break those shocks; crueler to deliver them.

All urgency is not ominous. If, like a religion, the telegram attends on death, it attends no less eagerly on love and birth. "A boy arrived this morning. Father and child doing well "— this is more frequently the tenor of the wire. And the wire may be the rapier of comedy. Do you remember Bernard Shaw's rebuff to Lady Randolph Churchill for asking him to dinner? He had the vegetarian view of eating his " fellow-creatures." He chided her for inviting a person of " my well-known habits." " Know nothing of your habits," came the blithe retort, " hope they're better than your manners."

The art of the telegram is threatened. Once we struggled to put our all in ten words — simple, at least, if not sensuous and passionate. Now the day-letter and night-letter lead us into garrulity. No transition from Greek to Byzantine could be worse than this. We should resist it. The time will doubtless come when our descendants will recall us as austere and frugal in our use of the telegram. But we should preserve this sign of our Spartan manhood. Let us defer the softness and effeminacy of long, cheap telegrams. Let us remain primitive, virginal, terse.

OF PLEASANT THINGS

WHEN I was a child we lived on the border of the town, and the road that passed our windows went in two ways. One branch ran up the hill under the old city gateway and out through the mean city "lanes." The other branch turned round our corner and ran into the countryside. Day and night many carts lumbered by our windows, in plain hearing. In the day-time I took no pleasure in them, but when I awoke at night and the thick silence was broken by the noise of a single deliberate cart it filled me with vague enchantment. I still feel this enchantment. The steady effort of the wheels, their rattle as they passed over the uneven road, their crunching deliberateness, gives me a sense of acute pleasure. That pleasure is at its highest when a solitary lantern swings underneath the wagon. In the old days the load might be coal, with the colliery-man sitting hunched on the driver's seat, a battered silhouette. Or the load might be from the brewery, making a start at dawn. Or it might be a load of singing harvest-women, hired in the market square by the sweet light of the morning. But not the wagon or the sight of the wagoner pleases me, so much as that honest, steady, homely sound coming through the vacancy of the night. I like it, I find it friendly and companionable, and I hope to like it till I die.

The city sounds improve with distance. Sometimes, in lazy summer evenings, I like the faint rumble, the growing roar, the receding rumble of the elevated, with the suggestion of its open windows and its passengers relaxed and indolent after the exhausting day. Always I like the moaning sounds from the river craft, carried so softly into the town. But New York sounds and Chicago sounds are usually discords. I hate bells — the sharp spinsterish telephone bell, the lugubrious church bell, the clangorous railway bell. Well, perhaps not the sleigh bell or the dinner bell.

I like the element of water. An imagist should write of the waters of Lake Michigan which circle around Mackinac Island: the word crystal is the hackneyed word for those pure lucent depths. When the sun shines on the bottom, every pebble is seen in a radiance of which the jewel is a happy memory. In Maine lakes and along the coast of Maine one has the same visual delight in water as clear as crystal, and on the coast of Ireland I have seen the Atlantic Ocean slumber in a glowing amethyst or thunder in a wall of emerald. On the southern shore of Long Island, who has not seen the sumptuous ultramarine, with a surf as snowy as apple-blossom? After shrill and meager New York, the color of that Atlantic is drenching.

The dancing harbor of New York is a beauty that never fades, but I hate the New York skyline except at night. In the day-time those punctured walls seem imbecile to me. They look out on the river with such a lidless, such an inhuman, stare. Nothing of man clings to them. They are barren as the rocks, empty as the deserted vaults of cliff-dwellers. A little wisp of white steam may suggest humanity, but not these bleak cliffs themselves. At night, however, they become human. They look out on the black moving river with marigold eyes. And Madison Square at nightfall has the same, or even a more ætherial, radiance. From the hurried streets the walls of light seem like a deluge of fairy splendor. This is always a gay transformation to the eye of the citydweller, who is forever oppressed by the ugliness around him.

Flowers are pleasant things to most people. I like flowers, but seldom cut flowers. The gathering of wild flowers seems to me unnecessarily wanton, and is it not hateful to, see people coming home with dejected branches of dogwood or broken autumn festoons or apple-blossoms already rusting in the train? I like flowers best in the fullness of the meadow or the solitude of a forsaken garden. Few things are so pleasant as to find oneself all alone in a garden that has, so to speak, drifted out to sea. The life that creeps up between its broken flagstones, the life that trails so impudently across the path, the life that spawns in the forgotten pond — this has a fascination beyond the hand of gardeners. Once I shared a neglected garden with an ancient turtle, ourselves the only living things within sight or sound. When the turtle wearied of sunning himself he shuffled to the artificial pond, and there he lazily paddled through waters laced down with scum. It was pleasant to see him, a not too clean turtle in waters not too clean. Perhaps if the family had been home the gardener would have scoured him.

Yet order is pleasant. If I were a millionaire —

which I thank heaven I am not, nor scarcely a millionth part of one — I should take pleasure in the silent orderliness that shadowed me through my home. Those invisible hands that patted out the pillows and shined the shoes and picked up everything, even the Sunday newspapers — those I should enjoy. I should enjoy especially the guardian angel who hid from me the casualties of the laundry and put the surviving laundry away. In heaven there is no laundry, or mending of laundry. For the millionaire the laundry is sent and the laundry is sorted away. Blessed be the name of the millionaire; I envy him little else. Except, perhaps, his linen sheets.

The greatest of all platitudes is the platitude that life is in the striving. Is this altogether true? I think not. Not for those menial offices so necessary to our decent existence, so little decent in their victims or themselves. But one does remember certain striving that brought with it almost instant happiness, like the reward of the child out coasting or the boy who has made good in a hard, grinding game. It is pleasant to think of one's first delicious surrender to fatigue after a long day's haul on a hot road. That surrender, in all one's joints, with all one's driven will, is the ecstasy that even the Puritan allowed himself. It is the nectar of the pioneer. In our civilization we take it away from the workers, as we take the honey from the bees — but I wish to think of things pleasant, not of our civilization. Fatigue of this golden kind is unlike the leaden fatigue of compulsion or of routine. It is the tang that means a man is young. If one gets it from games, even golf, I think it is pleasant. It is the great charm that Englishmen possess and understand.

These are ordinary pleasant things, not the pleasant things of the poet. They barely leave the hall of pleasant things. A true poet, I imagine, is one who captures in the swift net of his imagination the wild pleasantnesses and delights that to me would be flying presences quickly lost to view. But every man must bag what he can in his own net, whether he be rational or poetic. For myself, I have to use my imagination to keep from being snared by too many publicists and professors and persons of political intent. These are invaluable servants of humanity, admirable masters of our mundane institutions. But they fill the mind with *-ations*. They pave the meadows with concrete; they lose the free swing of pleasant things.

THE AVIATOR

So endlessly the gray-lipped sea
Kept me within his eye,
And lean he licked his hollow flanks
And followed up the sky.

I was the lark whose song was heard
When I was lost to sight,
I was the golden arrow loosed
To pierce the heart of night.

    I fled the little earth, I climbed
    Above the rising sun,
    I met the morning in a blaze
    Before my hour was gone.

I ran beyond the rim of space,
Its reins I flung aside,
Laughter was mine and mine was youth
And all my own was pride.

    So endlessly the gray-lipped sea
    Kept me within his eye,
    And lean he licked his hollow flanks
    And followed up the sky.

From end to end I knew the way,
I had no doubt or fear;

The minutes were a forfeit paid
To fetch the landfall near.

But all at once my heart I held,
My carol frozen died,
A white cloud laid her cheek to mine
And wove me to her side.

Her icy fingers clasped my flesh,
Her hair drooped in my face,
And up we fell and down we rose
And twisted into space.

So endlessly the gray-lipped sea
Kept me within his eye,
And lean he licked his hollow flanks
And followed up the sky.

Laughter was mine and mine was youth,
I pressed the edge of life,
I kissed the sun and raced the wind,
I found immortal strife.

Out of myself I spent myself,
I lost the mortal share,
My grave is in the ashen plain,
My spirit in the air.

Good-by, sweet pride of man that flew,
Sweet pain of man that bled,
I was the lark that spilled his heart,
The golden arrow sped.

So endlessly the gray-lipped sea
Kept me within his eye,
And lean he licked his hollow flanks
And followed up the sky.

THE END